MODEL UN HANDBOOK

A Preparation for MUN Conferences

Greg Hodgin

Hamilton Books
A member of
The Rowman & Littlefield Publishing Group
Lanham · Boulder · New York · Toronto · Plymouth, UK

Copyright © 2012 by
Hamilton Books
4501 Forbes Boulevard
Suite 200
Lanham, Maryland 20706
Hamilton Books Acquisitions Department (301) 459-3366

Estover Road
Plymouth PL6 7PY
United Kingdom

Library of Congress Control Number: 2011920282
ISBN: 978-0-7618-5449-4 (paperback : alk. paper)
eISBN: 978-0-7618-5450-0

CONTENTS

LIST OF TABLES

PREFACE

As a Model UN delegate, head delegate, coach and sponsor, time and again I have dealt with the inconvenient lack of a concise, well-written handbook that I could give to new delegates and sponsors. After fruitlessly searching for a book that was a one-stop source for Model UN information, I took notes for myself and my delegates, hoping that I could give them small pieces of concise information before going into committee. After a year of this, I realized that perhaps I should write the book I needed. You are now holding it. I truly hope you find this handbook useful and that it will eliminate for you many of the frustration that I experienced.

Greg Hodgin
Atlanta, Georgia
January, 2010

ACKNOWLEDGMENTS

A book like this does not just come into being. I would like to first thank Mrs. Peggy Fryer, who was my high school World History teacher. She was the one who first introduced me to Model UN with consequences for the rest of my days. Also, I would like to thank Dr. Rashid Naim, without the support of whom this book would not exist. Last, but not least, I would like to thank Tyra Bouhamdan for placing the final polish on this book and for being there when I needed her. All that is good in this book came about with her help; all mistakes are mine alone.

CHAPTER ONE

MODEL UN AT A GLANCE

Congratulations! If you've picked up this book, you are on your way to gaining a better understanding not only of the country in which you live, but also of how international policy and diplomacy is played out on the world stage. I personally hope you enjoy reading and using this resource as much as I enjoyed writing it.

What is Model UN?

Model UN stands for Model United Nations. Model United Nations is a simulation of the actual United Nations. Each school (whether a high school or college) will be assigned a country by a conference at which that school participates. High schools and colleges apply for these countries well in advance of the conference. Each conference has specific rules on country assignments and due dates for applications and the like. Your sponsor will be able to tell you the details for this scheduling. To apply for a conference, it is usually best to contact either its Secretary-General or the person in charge of assigning countries. The conference will usually have a list of countries represented and the committees on which they will be. It is vital to match the number of attending delegates with a country or countries that have a similar number represented at the conference. The students who are assigned that country will do research on it, learning its customs, history and foreign policy. Their country's foreign policy will be written up in what is known as a position paper, and sent to the conference beforehand.

At the actual conference, the team will represent delegates from their country to the United Nations. They will be expected to comport themselves as the actual delegates of that country. Their objective is to work with other countries in their committee and pass resolutions, which can be considered international law once passed. The conference conforms to a set of rules, known as 'parliamentary procedure', which help to facilitate active debate. It is imperative that these rules are understood so that the work of the team is not diminished. Some conferences award delegates and teams for outstanding work on position papers and for the country's performance at the conference.

What is the point of this?

Why should you participate in Model UN? There are a number of answers to this question. First and foremost, you will learn about international affairs and how the international system works. That might sound boring, but it really is not. Think about this: how many times have you turned on the news and seen an event happening hundreds or even thousands of miles away that has nothing to do with your country? Have you ever wondered about why something is happening in that location? Or why those people are fighting over whatever cause concerns them? Why can't they just work it out? Model UN can help you understand why these people are in conflict, what the international community is doing about it, and what you can do to help the situation.

Model UN teaches you skills that you can use not only in high school or college, but for the rest of your life. Do you want to win an argument? Model UN can help; you must learn to debate effectively to succeed. We live in a society that involves centralized bureaucracies; Model UN can help you understand how to get involved in and influence society. How do we deal with people we don't like? Again, Model UN teaches you how to manage people with whom you simply don't get along. You will go through life and sooner or later you will meet someone that you don't like but you must work or deal with. Model UN can help you not only deal with these people, but also sometimes convince them of your views or simply learn to coexist with them without conflict. Do you like it when people agree with you? Model UN can hone your persuasion skills and help you influence people.

How will this handbook help me?

This book is set up so that this will be all you need for a successful Model UN experience. The next chapter introduces the history of the UN, from its formation in 1945 to the present day. Chapter Three presents the "alphabet soup" of the UN: i.e. common UN abbreviations and what they designate, and the structure of the UN. Chapter Four explains position papers: papers that are written before a conference to show that the team understands their country's position. Chapter Five describes parliamentary procedure and how to use the rules of Model UN to your advantage. Chapter Six describes exactly how to control a committee and gives tactical advice on gaining leadership skills. Chapter Seven covers effective public speaking tactics. Chapter Eight covers what a resolution is and how to write an effective one. Chapter Nine explains the intricacies of voting procedure and how to use these rules to your advantage for passing your resolution. Chapter Ten gives advice on how and where to conduct your research for your conference assignment. At the very end are three Appendices of basic United Nations documents that you will find very useful. In short, this handbook holds everything that you will need to be successful at conference, in the order that you will usually need it.

CHAPTER TWO

THE HISTORY OF THE UNITED NATIONS

Before we can get started on Model UN, it is a good idea to make sure that you have a full knowledge of the actual United Nations. This chapter will cover the history of the UN and its predecessor, the League of Nations.

What was the League of Nations, and why did it fail?

World War I: Causes and Effects

World War I was the most destructive conflict in human history when it took place. The issues that caused this war were very complex and an entire book could be written about just that, but some review of the causes is in order.

In the early 20th century, the entire continent of Europe was poised on the brink of war, but most of the main combatants did not know it. France was angry with Germany for the Franco-Prussian War of 1871 where Germany had taken Alsace-Lorraine from the French, and the French vowed revenge. England was angry with Germany due to Germany's building a navy that could challenge England's supremacy of the high seas. Germany was angry that during the colonization of Africa it was nearly cut out of the negotiations, and therefore felt sidelined by the other colonial powers, forcing it to seek an alliance with Austria-Hungary, a country which wished to direct its problems outward as it was beginning to dissipate internally. The complex ring of treaties that had been signed by the Great Powers and the minor powers forced the entire continent into a series of interlocking agreements wherein if one small country declared war on another, they would be able to call on their accords to force other, larger countries into the conflict. This would lead to a domino effect where any small country that was attacked would immediately drag all of Europe down with it, which is exactly what happened in 1914.

In 1914, the massive set of treaties and negotiations dragged the entire continent into war. On June 28, 1914, a Serbian assassin shot Archduke Franz Ferdinand, heir to the throne of Austria-Hungary. Within two months, the entire continent was at war. Unfortunately for all involved, most of the leaders of the Great Powers assumed that the war would be over quickly, the "Victory before Christmas." This was unfortunately not the case.

Germany was sandwiched between two belligerent powers: the French and the Russians. The Germans realized this, and had come up with a bold idea called the Schlieffen Plan: attack France and knock it out of the war quickly, before Russia had a chance to mobilize its troops. The Germans quickly ran through neutral Belgium and started to march on France towards Paris. The Schlieffen Plan was working incredibly well. Unfortunately for the Germans, the Russians mobilized faster than anticipated, which forced Germany to divert troops to its Eastern Front. This caused the German drive to Paris to stall about 20 miles from that city, ultimately to be thrown back; forcing them to seek a hole in the defenses and making them race Northbound towards the sea in an attempt to outflank the Allied forces. This strategy ultimately failed, leading to two lines of opposing armies, both of whom lacked the ability to break each other's lines. Due to the invention of the machine gun and other technological advances, it was far easier to defend a territory than to attack it. Military commanders had not fully grasped this concept, however, and sent hundreds of thousands of men to needlessly die on barbed wire in No Man's Land.

Finally, in 1917, the Russian government collapsed. By this point, America had entered the war on the side of the Allies (England, France and Russia) against the Central Powers (Austria-Hungary and Germany). The Russian army collapsed, allowing the Germans to shift their battle-hardened troops to the Western Front to force a breakthrough. The Western Front line broke again, and the Germans drove towards Paris for the second time. The Alliance force was able to stop the invasion and turned the tide against the Germans. The German Army, after four years of fighting, simply could not take anymore. Germany was invaded, and the German Kaiser abdicated. Austria-Hungary also collapsed, leading to the dissolution of the Central Powers. The armistice was declared on November 11, 1918.

Versailles: Causes and Effects

After the war, the four Great Powers who won the war—Italy, France, England and the United States—began crafting a peace treaty. Woodrow Wilson came to France as a hero; his Fourteen Points were hailed as a way for the Germans to have a fair and just peace. Wilson's Fourteen Points were a promise to the defeated countries that the peace that was secured on the battlefield would be just. The most important part of his Fourteen Points for this handbook was Wilson's idea of an international organization dedicated to the eradication of war. However, the French and British would have none of it. They had fought the war the hardest and longest; they wanted to make sure that Germany would never be able to attack them again. Because of this, the Treaty of Versailles really satisfied no one and laid the groundwork for World War II.

The Versailles Treaty imposed very harsh conditions on Germany. Germany was forced to give Alsace-Lorraine to France. Its Air Force ceased to exist, and its Army could only have 100,000 soldiers. Germany was forced to pay reparations for the war which added up to an amount so astronomically high that if Germany had actually paid the entire sum, they would have paid until 1984.

Austria-Hungary was broken up into a number of constituent countries which also led to problems further down the road. The infamous 'War Guilt Clause' made Germany the sole responsible party for the entire war, a bitter pill for the Germans to swallow. More importantly, Versailles also set up an international organization for the discussion and promotion of international peace. That organization was the League of Nations, the predecessor to the United Nations. Unfortunately for all involved, the United States Senate failed to ratify Versailles, and chose not to join the League of Nations. Because of this, the League was significantly weak from the time of its inception.

The League of Nations

The League of Nations was set up in order to resolve any international issues that may arise. The first official act of the League was to ratify Versailles, thereby technically ending World War I. The League had three organs: the Secretariat, the Council and the Assembly. The Secretariat was responsible for preparing reports and agendas for the League. The Council was analogous to the UN Security Council in that it was charged with peacekeeping. The Assembly was akin the UN General Assembly. However, a unanimous vote was required to pass any resolution, leading to very little being accomplished. Clearly, this led to problems further down the road.

The League ultimately failed; however, it did have some notable successes, including the Mandate system. The mandate system was where former colonies were governed by other countries until those colonies were able to govern themselves; mandates were passed on to the UN Trusteeship Council. The League also managed to settle a large number of international disputes in the 1920's and 1930's.

The Failure of the League of Nations

There were some major problems with the League of Nations. First, the League had to have a unanimous decision within the Council, often a difficult goal to attain. Secondly, one of the world's Great Powers, the United States, failed to join. Thirdly, the League had no true way to enforce its will; it had no standing army at all. Instead, the organization was forced to rely on economic sanctions.

Because of this, the League rapidly lost influence in the 1930's. When the Japanese invaded Manchuria, the League condemned it. Japan simply left the League. In 1935, Italy invaded Ethiopia. The Ethiopian Emperor, Haile Selassie, came to the League to make an impassioned speech for help in freeing his homeland. The League sanctioned Italy, but could take no other action. Adolph Hitler came to power in Germany, re-annexed territory and began rebuilding the army. The League condemned this, but did nothing to stop it. By 1939, war was clearly on the way in Europe, and the League unfortunately had failed to prevent it. It was clear that a new and more powerful organization was required to deal with the international community.

What happened during World War II that led up to the creation of the United Nations?

On September 1, 1939, Germany invaded Poland, precipitating World War II. The European powers had finally realized that Hitler could only be stopped through force of arms, leading to France and England declaring war on Germany. Germany responded in the spring of 1940 by nearly destroying all of the English and French armies and completely defeating France. However, the English and French were able to evacuate most of their troops at a small port in Northern France called Dunkirk. This would come back to haunt Hitler later. In a bit of historical irony, Hitler forced France to sign the armistice in the same railcar that was used during the signing of the World War I armistice. At this point, Hitler attempted to bomb England into submission. The Battle of Britain ended with Hitler's Air Force, the Luftwaffe, beaten back across the Channel. Without air supremacy, it was impossible to invade England.

The tide began to turn for the Germans when, in 1941, the United States entered the war after the Japanese attack on Pearl Harbor. On January 1, 1942, the Declaration by United Nations was signed by 26 countries, wherein these countries promised to not sign a separate peace with the Axis powers (Germany, Japan and Italy) and to uphold the Atlantic Charter, which included a number of UN principles. This was the first step toward the United Nations as we know it.

Hitler decided to take the initiative with the Soviet Union and invaded it, hoping to quickly eliminate it as a threat before it decided to attack him. Although he initially met with success, the Russians threw their worst weapon at him: the harsh Russian winter. Hitler decided to stay and fight it out, leading to his armies being decimated by cold and disease. The Russians were able to slowly push the Germans back. After this point, the Germans lost the initiative in the war and were fighting on the defensive from then on.

On June 6, 1944, the Allied armies invaded France during Operation Overlord, also known as D-Day. Germany was thrown back, and it looked to all as if the Germans might finally be defeated. In August, 1944, leaders of the US, UK, China and the USSR sat down at Dumbarton Oaks, Washington, D.C., to discuss the new organization that would supplant the League of Nations. Finally, on May 2, 1945, the Germans surrendered. It was clear to all involved that a war of this magnitude must never be allowed to happen again.

When was the United Nations founded, and how did it happen?

On October 24, 1945 in San Francisco, the United Nations Charter was ratified by the permanent five members of the Security Council (P5) and by a majority of the 46 signatories. The United Nations Charter stated that the purpose of the UN was to prevent future world wars and to ensure international peace. The UN took over all League of Nations mandates and transferred control to the Trusteeship Council. The League formally dissolved in 1946.

When the UN was formed, were there any beginning conflicts?

The UN was formed in 1945, and within a few years two very large con-
flicts raised their heads, the first being the independence of Israel, and the
second being the conflict between India and Pakistan.

The Independence of Israel

The Israeli question was the first serious test of the new United Nations.
The UN inherited this problem from the League, which had failed to resolve the
issue. The challenge at hand was how to partition, if at all, two disparate
peoples: the Palestinians and the Israelis. Both felt that the other had encroached
on their land, and compromise was out of the question. The issue was brought
before the United Nations.
   The UN decided in 1947 to partition the land. A part of it would go to a new
Jewish state: Israel. The second part would go to the Palestinians. This was elu-
cidated in General Assembly Resolution 181. Israel acquiesced, and the country
of Israel was born on May 14, 1948. Before this, however, the Arab nations did
not want Israel to exist, so they attacked the nascent country. Israel managed to
fight its way to victory, and the UN managed to broker a ceasefire between
Israel and the Arab nations. This led to the first UN peacekeeping force deployed in Israel in 1948 and remaining in place to this day.

Kashmir

In 1947, Great Britain left India to its own devices. The dream of Gandhi
had been fulfilled: India was granted its independence. However, instead of one
large India, there were two countries produced: India and Pakistan. Pakistan was
formed from the largely Muslim population of British India, while India proper
was formed from a largely Hindu population. A territory called Kashmir was in
between India and Pakistan, both of which laid claim to it, and immediately began fighting each other over it. The war wound down in 1949, and the UN was
called in to observe and enforce the ceasefire. This peacekeeping force remains
present to this day.

What was that whole Korea thing, anyway? I thought that was just the US!

In 1950, a civil war broke out between North Korea and South Korea. This
quickly turned into the first test between the Soviet Union, China and the United
States. When the fighting broke out, the issue was taken to the UN. The Soviet
Union was boycotting the Security Council at this point (due to the fact that the
UN recognized Taiwan as the Republic of China and gave the seat that the
USSR thought belonged to the People's Republic of China to Taiwan instead),
so the USSR was unable to use its veto to stop the UN from taking up arms in
defense of South Korea. What is known as the Korean War was therefore fought
under the UN flag and under UN command. Realizing the mistake they had
made, the Soviets retook their Security Council seat and vetoed any other reso-

lutions dealing with the Korean situation. The United States and its allies took the question to the General Assembly, which passed UNGA Resolution 377, also known as the "Uniting for Peace" Resolution. In essence, this resolution gave the General Assembly the ability to take up issues of international peace and security if the Security Council was "deadlocked." The Korean conflict lasted until 1953 when an armistice was signed. At press time for this book North Korea and South Korea are still technically at war, although there is no actual fighting, since a peace treaty to formally end the war has not been signed.

What role did the UN play during the Cold War?

During the Cold War, the United Nations played a significant role as a neutral arbiter in disputes that did not directly involve the superpowers (the United States and the Soviet Union).

The UN's first major challenge to international peace and security came in 1956 during the Suez crisis. The Suez Canal was nationalized by the Egyptian government, leading France and Great Britain (both still colonial powers at this point) to step up their support of Israel who attacked Egypt with their reinforcement. The situation was brought to the Security Council, where both France and the UK vetoed any resolution dealing with the situation. The United States did not want this conflict to continue (from a Cold War perspective, it was destabilizing as it could have led to the spread of communism in that region). Because of this, the United States invoked the Uniting for Peace Resolution passed in 1950, calling a "special session" of the General Assembly to discuss the issue. This was necessary as the Security Council was obviously deadlocked, since two of the permanent five members were vetoing anything dealing with the crisis. Then Canadian diplomat Lester Pearson suggested to the United Nations that a United Nations Emergency Force (UNEF) be sent to the region with the consent of the conflicting parties to "hold the line" while the belligerents work out a peace settlement. This suggestion was taken into account, and UNEF I was deployed with neutral forces to stabilize the region. This led to Pearson being awarded the Nobel Peace Prize in 1957 and also led to the actual creation of United Nations peacekeeping.

The UN engaged in classic peacekeeping up to the end of the Cold War. However, it was clear that the P5 would not allow large scale peacekeeping to take place. Although peacekeeping was relegated to the sidelines, the UN engaged in a number of other missions consistent with its mandate: specifically, pushing universal human rights standards, women's rights, (by the 1970s) the environment, children's rights, and in one of the most successful UN stories, health issues with the World Health Organization (WHO) eliminating smallpox in December 1979.

After the end of the Cold War, what did the UN do?

With the dissolution of the Soviet Union, many countries turned to the UN to have a greater role in global governance. Up until the disintegration of the USSR, the UN had only been in the business of relatively tranquil peacekeeping (with the exceptions of Korea in 1950 and the United Nations Operation in the Congo, ONUC, in the 1960's). As one of the superpowers dissolved into numerous smaller territories, the UN was tasked with controlling the flare-ups which took place at the end of the Cold War, with the UN peacekeeping system stretched far beyond its original design. Although the international community had very high hopes for the UN, the Member States chose to not fully fund or give the organization the personnel required to actually engage in the tasks that the Member States asked of it. This led to the UN being asked to do far more than it possibly could, making it appear ineffective. The UN failed to stop the Rwandan genocide (1994) and did not prevent the Srebrenica massacre (1995). By this point, it was considered a marginal player in world politics and was near bankruptcy, practically collapsing from debt. The UN, however, began to engage in reforming its peacekeeping system and began to reapportion the debt that Member states owed to it. To this day, the UN continues to carry a debt that is far from manageable.

How has the UN dealt with 9/11, terrorism and the US invasion of Iraq?

The UN Security Council (UNSC) passed a number of resolutions after the September 11, 2001 attacks on the World Trade Center and the Pentagon specifically condemning them and authorizing the creation of a counter-terrorism subcommittee that reports directly to the UNSC. The UNSC also gave the US-led coalition the green light to attack the Taliban in Afghanistan, and a mandate to engage in nation-building in that country. All of these decisions were direct results of the September 11 attacks on the United States. The UN has been very active in Afghanistan but not on a peacekeeping level; instead, the UN has dealt with human rights and women's rights issues, as well as post-conflict nation building.

The US invasion of Iraq was not authorized by the UN Security Council. The US decided to invade Iraq without the mandate of the UN Security Council. Although US-led coalition forces successfully invaded Iraq and engaged in regime change, the US-led coalition underestimated the tenacity of resistance to a US-backed government and failed to anticipate the complications of its occupation. The UN did send civilian staff to help with reconstruction; however, after an attack on the main UN compound in Baghdad in 2003, the UN withdrew its staff, leaving the US completely alone in Iraq.

What does the future hold for the UN?

The future of the UN is in the hands of its Member states and in people like you. The UN was set up specifically to deal with the entirety of the world's problems: it is up to future generations to realize these far-sighted dreams. In Model UN, you will be charting that future in committee.

CHAPTER THREE

THE STRUCTURE OF THE UNITED NATIONS

In this chapter, we look at the structure of the United Nations. It is vital to understand how the international body works; without knowing how it works, how can you use it?

What are the main organs of the UN?

The United Nations has six major organs. The following is a list of the organs in the order in which they are discussed in the Charter and the Articles under which they are defined.

1. ***The General Assembly (GA)*** (Articles 9 to 22). The General Assembly is possibly the closest that the international community has come to a "world parliament;" every Member state has a seat in the General Assembly and every Member has the opportunity to speak and vote. At the time of this writing, the United Nations has 192 Members, thereby meaning that the General Assembly has 192 voting Members. In addition to the 192 Members, two others have Observer status—they have seats but are unable to vote on substantive resolutions: the Holy See (the Vatican) and Palestine.

2. ***The Security Council (UNSC)*** (Articles 23 to 32). The Security Council is comprised of 15 Members of which five are permanent members (P5): The United States of America, France, The United Kingdom of Great Britain and Northern Ireland, the Republic of China (this seat was taken by the People's Republic of China in 1971)[1] and the Union of Soviet Socialist Republics (USSR, this seat was taken by the Russian Federation in 1991 after the dissolution of the USSR).[2] The other 10 Members are voted in for two year terms by the General Assembly. The Security Council is the main body which deals with international peace and security.

3. ***The Economic and Social Council (ECOSOC)*** (Articles 61to 72). The Economic and Social Council consists of 54 Members of the United Nations who are elected by the General Assembly to serve three year

terms. ECOSOC deals with economic, social and environmental aspects of the international system, and will be discussed further below.

4. ***The Trusteeship Council*** (Articles 86 to 91). As of 1994, the Trusteeship Council suspended operations; however it remains an organ of the UN Charter, although it is considered dormant. The Trusteeship Council, as of the time of this writing, has five members: the permanent five members of the UNSC. The Trusteeship Council was tasked with decolonization, which was ultimately successful. With its mission completed, the Trusteeship Council was suspended.

5. ***The International Court of Justice (ICJ)*** (Articles 92 to 96 and the International Court of Justice Statute). The International Court of Justice could be considered a part of the judicial branch of the United Nations;[3] the ICJ only hears cases bought to it by Members states who agree to its jurisdiction. It does not hear cases from individuals or state citizens. The Statute of the ICJ, in Appendix B, gives more details into judge selection and the inner workings of the court.

6. ***Secretariat*** (Articles 97 to 101). The Secretariat is the civil service administration of the United Nations, culminating in the office of the Secretary-General, and it is considered to be the *de facto* leader of the United Nations. The Secretariat is the organ which conducts the day-to-day activities of the United Nations.

Who has what powers in the UN?

Listed here are the five active organs of the United Nations, specifically the responsibilities and powers of each organ with references to the relevant sections of the Charter.

General Assembly: The GA can and does discuss literally any issue (Articles 10 and 11), may make recommendations and conduct studies (Article 13) and also approve trusteeship agreements (Article 16). The only stipulation on the GA is that it cannot discuss any matter that the Security Council is discussing unless the Security Council so asks (Article 12). The GA also has the ability to consider and approve the budget of the United Nations (Article 17, Section 1). In addition, the GA approves the following with a two-thirds majority of those Members present and voting: recommendations with respect to international peace and security, the election of the non-permanent members of the Security Council, the election of the members of the Economic and Social Council, the election of members of the Trusteeship Council, the admission of new Members to the United Nations (this is stipulated in Article 4, Section 2 detailing that the Security Council must recommend the new Member to the General Assembly), the suspension of the rights and privileges of membership (this is stipulated in Article 5, specifically that the Security Council must recommend the expulsion), the expulsion of Members (this is stipulated in Article 6, again with the recommendation of the Security Council), questions relating to the operation of the trusteeship system and budgetary questions (all of these stipulations are listed in Article 18, Section 2). The GA may also strip a Member of its vote if it is in arrears with its payments for two full years (Article 19). The General Assembly may also establish any subsidiary organs as it sees fit (Article 22). The GA may ask the International Court of Justice for an advisory opinion on any legal matter (Article 96, Section 1). It appoints the Secretary-General upon the recommendation of the Security Council (Article 97). Also the General Assembly can adopt amendments to the United Nations Charter with a two-thirds majority of the Members of the General Assembly including all of the permanent members of the Security Council (Article 108).

The Security Council: The Security Council is tasked with the primary responsibility for the maintenance of international peace and security (Article 24, Section 1). Security Council resolutions are binding; i.e. they must be followed by the Members of the United Nations (Article 25). Any decision made by the SC must be made with nine affirmative votes and no negative votes from the permanent five Members of the Security Council (Article 27, Sections 2 and 3). The Security Council is designed to function continuously and can meet anywhere in the world if the need so arises (Article 28). Like the General Assembly, it has the ability to establish subsidiary organs as it sees fit (Article 29). As stated above this organ also recommends new Members to the GA, expulsion if so required and who the Secretary-General will be. It may also request that the International Court of Justice give an advisory opinion when the SC sees fit (Article 96, Section 1), and it has the power, if requested, to enforce ICJ decisions (Article 94, Section 2). The Security Council, as opposed to the Trusteeship Council, has jurisdiction over what the UN may consider strategic areas at any given time (Article 83).

Due to the Security Council's responsibility towards international peace and security, there are three more Chapters in the Charter stipulating its powers and responsibilities (Chapters VI-VIII). Chapter VI deals with Pacific Settlement of Disputes, wherein the Security Council recommends non-invasive methods to resolving situations dealing with international peace and security. These methods usually involve the consent of both parties involved.

Chapter VII is considered the most important of these four Chapters with respect to the Security Council. If a substantive resolution is passed under Chapter VII stipulations, the Security Council has the power to ask for and enforce economic sanctions and other non-military means of persuasion (Articles 40 and 41) and may also use "any means necessary" to restore the peace if all else fails (Article 42). In essence, the Security Council can invade and occupy a country if that country is deemed to be disturbing international peace and security. The Members of the United Nations are responsible for providing the Security Council with the troops required to effectively enforce its resolutions (Article 43 and Article 49). However, if a Member is attacked, that Member has the complete right to self-defense (Article 51).

The traditional idea of United Nations peacekeeping actually falls in between Chapter VI and Chapter VII. Technically, there is no such concept as peacekeeping in the UN Charter and the Charter has been "stretched" to accommodate the demands of peacekeeping (Articles 37 and 38). Peacekeeping is also sometimes known as "Chapter VI and a half" due to its ambiguous nature in the Charter.

Chapter VIII deals with regional arrangements with respect to international peace and security. The key article here is Article 53 which states that "No enforcement action shall be taken under regional arrangements or by regional agencies without the authorization of the Security Council." This Article therefore makes all regional organizations subservient to the Security Council.

Economic and Social Council: The Economic and Social Council has the ability to initiate studies and/or reports on international economic, social, cultural, educational, health and related matters and may make recommendations on any such matters to the General Assembly as a whole, any individual Member or members of the United Nations and to the specialized agencies concerned (Article 62, Section 1). ECOSOC may make recommendations with respect to the purpose of human rights and fundamental freedoms for all (Article 62, Section 2) and may also prepare draft resolutions for the General Assembly with respect to matters falling within its competence (Article 62, Section 3). In addition, it may call international conferences on matters falling within its areas of expertise (Article 62, Section 4).

ECOSOC is the main organ of the United Nations that has the ability to work with Non-Governmental Organizations (NGOs) and other non-Members, as detailed in Articles 57 and 63, respectively. This organ may also request and obtain regular reports from specialized agencies on matters falling within its competence (Article 64, Section 1). Like the GA and the Security Council, ECOSOC has the ability to set up commissions for the performance of its functions (Article 68). It has the ability to invite Members who are not on ECOSOC to its deliberations (Article 69). However its most important function is contained in Article 71, which gives ECOSOC the ability to consult with NGOs if those NGOs are concerned with matters within its aptitude. This allows ECOSOC to tap into the vast array of transnational organizations for new concepts.

International Court of Justice: The International Court of Justice is considered the principal judicial organ of the United Nations and has a statute attached to the UN Charter for its operation (Article 92). Every Member of the United Nations agrees to comply with the decisions of the ICJ (Article 94, Section 1). If one of the parties in question fails to uphold the decision of the ICJ, any other party concerned may request that the Security Council take measures to enforce that judgment (Article 94, Section 2). There are two types of opinions: contentious and advisory. Contentious opinions involve two Members bringing an issue to the ICJ and are covered under Article 94. An advisory opinion is requested by one of the other organs of the United Nations and is not binding; however, they do carry a large amount of weight within the UN System. The General Assembly and the Security Council may request advisory opinions from the ICJ (Article 96, Section 1). The General Assembly may also authorize other organs and specialized agencies to request advisory opinions from this court (Article 96, Section 2).

Secretariat: The Secretariat is composed of the Secretary-General (SG) and the UN staff. The SG is considered to be the chief administrative officer of the Organization (Article 97). He acts in the capacity of the chief administrative officer for the GA, the SC, ECOSOC and the Trusteeship Council and he makes an annual report to the General Assembly on the work of the Organization (Article 98). The SG may bring to the attention of the Security Council any matters which may threaten the maintenance of international peace and security (Article 99). The Secretariat should not receive any instructions from any external authority with respect to the Organization (Article 100, Section 1) and each Member must respect the international character of the Secretariat and not politically influence them with respect to their responsibilities (Article 100, Section 2). The staff of the Secretariat is appointed by the Secretary-General under guidelines established by the GA (Article 101, Section 1). The staff of the Secretariat is selected based on efficiency, competence and integrity, with due attention paid to recruiting staff from as wide a geographic basis as possible (Article 101, Section 3).

The Trusteeship Council: Although the Trusteeship Council is dormant, a short review of its former functions is in order. This organ was set up specifically to help with the decolonization effort already under way at the end of the Second World War. Chapter XII of the Charter goes into the specifics of the Trusteeship system; specifically the objectives (Article 76), what territories fall under its responsibility (Article 77), and which territories do not (Article 83). The Trusteeship Council is responsible for preparing reports, accepting petitions and providing for visits to the trust territories (Article 87). This council is also required to prepare an annual report on the trust territories for the General Assembly by means of a questionnaire on the advancement of the inhabitants of each such territory (Article 88).

What is the "Alphabet Soup" of the UN?

This is a list of commonly used acronyms within the United Nations system. Memorization of these terms is highly recommended: they are used time and again in most UN literature. Not all of these organizations are directly a part of the UN System; however they do report to one of the main organs of the UN. This is not a complete list, but it is a good place to start. The committees that are represented at most conferences are marked with an asterisk at the end. This does not mean that every Model UN conference has every committee marked by an asterisk; rather it means that these committees are more often than not represented at conferences. Also, please remember that each peacekeeping operation is given its own acronym and is not listed here: instead, go to the United

Nations Security Council webpage and access the current list of peacekeeping operations.

- ASEAN: Association of Southeast Asian Nations
- AU: African Union (*)
- CSD: Commission on Sustainable Development
- CSW: Commission on the Status of Women (*)
- DISEC: General Assembly First Committee, or "GA 1st" (Disarmament and International Security) (*)
- DPKO: Department of Peacekeeping Operations
- ECA: Economic Commission for Africa
- ECE: Economic Commission for Europe
- ECLAC: Economic Commission for Latin America and the Caribbean
- ECOFIN: General Assembly Second Committee, or "GA 2nd" (Economic and Financial) (*)
- ESCAP: Economic and Social Committee for Asia and the Pacific
- ESCWA: Economic and Social Committee for Western Asia
- EU: European Union
- FAO: Food and Agricultural Organization (*)
- GA 5th: General Assembly Fifth Committee (Administrative and Budgetary)
- GA 6th: General Assembly Sixth Committee (Legal) (*)
- GA Plen: General Assembly Plenary (*)
- IAEA: International Atomic Energy Agency (*)
- ICC: International Criminal Court
- ICJ: International Court of Justice
- ICTR: International Criminal Tribunal for Rwanda
- ICTY: International Criminal Tribunal for the former Yugoslavia
- ILO: International Labor Organization (*)
- IMF: International Monetary Fund
- MSC: Military Staff Committee
- NATO: North Atlantic Treaty Organization
- OAS: Organization of American States (*)
- OIC: Organization of the Islamic Conference (*)
- OSG: Office of the Secretary-General
- SOCHUM: General Assembly Third Committee, or "GA 3rd" (Social and Humanitarian) (*)
- SPECPOL: General Assembly Fourth Committee, or "GA 4th" (Special Political and Decolonization) (*)
- UNAIDS: Joint United Nations Programme on HIV/AIDS (*)
- UNCTAD: United Nations Conference on Trade and Development (*)
- UNDCP: United Nations Drug Control Programme
- UNDP: United Nations Development Programme (*)
- UNEP: United Nations Environmental Programme (*)

- UNESCO: United Nations Educational, Social and Cultural Organization (*)
- UNFPA: United Nations Fund for Population Activities
- UN-HABITAT: United Nations Human Settlements Programme
- UNHCR: United Nations High Commissioner for Refugees (*)
- UNHRC: United Nations Human Rights Council (*)
- UNICEF: United Nations Children's Fund
- UNRWA: United Nations Relief and Works Agency for Palestine Refugees in the Near East
- UNSC: United Nations Security Council (*)
- WFP: World Food Programme
- WHO: World Health Organization (*)
- WIPO: World Intellectual Property Organization
- WTO: World Trade Organization

How does the UN get its funding and where do UN troops come from?

The United Nations does not have the ability to tax its Members. There is no global tax in any way, shape or form in the international system. Instead, the United Nations procures funds in two ways: voluntary contributions from the Members and contributions as apportioned by the General Assembly (Article 17, Section 2).

The United Nations does not have a standing army. Instead, the Security Council reaches agreements with Members to garner troops, supplies, equipment, rights of passage and so on for the maintenance of international peace and security (Article 43).

Chapter Review

1. How many members compose each of the following organs: a) Security Council, b) ECOSOC, and c) General Assembly?

2. Name seven specific powers granted to the Security Council in the Charter?

3. Name five specific powers granted to ECOSOC in the Charter?

4. What organ of the UN do NGOS have the ability to report to?

5. Where are the United Nations' armed forces located?

CHAPTER FOUR

POSITION PAPERS

Before a Model UN conference begins, a position paper usually must be written on your country's policy. This chapter will walk you through the steps towards and reasons for writing a position paper.

What is a position paper?

A position paper is a short paper (usually two to three pages in length), which details a country's position on the topics being discussed in the committee in question. These position papers are turned in before the beginning of the conference; generally one to two months prior in order for the staff of the conference to read them in advance. Each committee's dais, which is composed of the chair, the assistant chair, the director, and/or the assistant director, writes a background guide, detailing the two to four topics that the committee will address. The position paper is your Member state's position on these topics. In other words, this could be considered your country's official dossier of exactly what your country believes with regards to each of these topics.

For instance, let's say that your country is Madagascar, which is an island nation, and one of the topics is the impact of global warming. More than likely, your position paper would involve stricter regulations on global warming due to the fact that it is well within your country's policy to push for greater limitations on climate change (otherwise your country could be potentially destroyed by this environmental pandemic).

What's the purpose of these papers?

Position papers are vital for the success of a team at any conference. They help a delegation prepare for the conference by motivating them to conduct research on their country and on their topics. It is impossible to write a good position paper without doing adequate research on both the country and the issue concerning it. Secondly, it provides an excellent template for resolution writing in committee. If someone has a question about policy and what the committee needs to address, to secure your vote, your position paper should give a general idea of exactly what you want with respect to the topic in question.

Most importantly, position papers are used by the dais to get a first approximation of how the delegation is prepared. The dais reads every position paper before the conference and walks into the conference with that position paper as their first impression. This is a golden opportunity for your delegation to score quick points with the dais, so be sure to write excellent position papers!

How do I write one and can I see a sample position paper?

To write an effective position paper, remember two basic features: language and efficiency. Position papers are not written in the vernacular; instead they use formal language. For instance, the first time that your country is mentioned, state the entire name of your country. China would be the People's Republic of China; the US would be the United States of America, and so on. After the first formal use of the country's name, it is acceptable to use the informal name, like China or Russia. However, there are no abbreviations. Therefore, it is not acceptable to say "The US." Instead, use the United States. Most position papers are at most two pages with no more than two-thirds of a page devoted to each topic. Each topic should begin with a general history of the issue, what the specific *Member state* has done to deal with the problem at hand, and finally and most importantly, what the Member state wants *the committee* to do to deal with the problem. The key here is efficiency: if the dais asks for two pages, they will only read two pages and ignore the rest. Usually, position papers are written using footnotes. However, this varies by conference, so be sure to check with the conference your team is attending for formatting questions prior to submitting your paper.

The following is a position paper presented at a former National Model United Nations conference. Remember: each conference has different rules for layout so check with the conference on exactly how their position papers must be written. Notice the emphasis on formal language.

Position Paper for the General Assembly Plenary

The Republic of Djibouti looks forward to working closely with its numerous regional allies in the African Union and the League of Arab States, along with the entire United Nations, to achieve lasting solutions to the complex issues before the General Assembly Plenary. Djibouti is confident that this committee can resolve these issues both in a regional and global manner.

I.   The Promotion of Alternative Sources of Energy

Alternative sources of energy are the future, and the Republic of Djibouti considers itself a regional and international pioneer in the alternative energy frontier. By partnering with Icelandic company Reykjavik Energy Invest [REI] Djibouti is set to be the site for "USD 5 million in research on the potential of geothermal resources in the area."[4] As a member and supporter of various existing efforts promoting alternative sources of energy, such as the Intergovernmental Panel on Climate Change [IPCC] and the Kyoto Protocol, Djibouti is proactively committed to promoting good environmental practices. The General Assembly must advocate efficiency and further organization in established structures by promoting stronger communication between states, transnational advocacy networks, the scientific community, and civil society. For example, projects by the Solar Electric Light Fund [SELF] established in developing nations are bringing the ability to run electricity directly to local peoples. However, noting the devastating historical exploitation of African resources, and further noting the finite nature and non-renewability of energy sources, Djibouti maintains that the foundations of development and construction of the African and global energy needs we are building today create opportunities for renewable energy for our future. According to the report on Renewable Energy in Africa, "only about 7% of Africa's enormous hydro potential has been harnessed....geothermal potential stands at 9000 MW but only about 60 MW has been exploited."[5] Given these statistics, there is no reason not to invest in funding of these renewable energy technologies. The Republic of Djibouti feels that every sovereign state is capable of independently making decisions about energy sources they choose to employ and that alternative sources of energy should not be forced upon any state, nor should they drastically harm the economies of such states. The UN must adopt the role of providing each state with an equal opportunity to access to alternative energy resources and technologies. It most importantly involves leveling the privileges and inequalities of certain member states over others, a problem especially relevant to Africa and one which this Assembly has not adequately addressed in the context of sustainable energy. Djibouti firmly believes that the stability of African infrastructures such as the African Union can be achieved through combined efforts of debt relief, strengthened regional coalition, and a shift in international investments and trade in the Horn of Africa region from non-renewable resources to a more sustainable medium, such as alternative energy sources. As businesses begin to capitalize on the upcoming industry of alternative energy production, it is crucial for the UN to support developing nations in their pursuit of clean, inexpensive and sustainable energy.

II. Breaking the Link Between Diamonds and Armed Conflict

The Republic of Djibouti recognizes with great appreciation the diligent work of the international community to address the issue of conflict diamonds and their link to armed conflict. Defined as "rough diamonds which are used by rebel movements to finance their military activities, including attempts to undermine or overthrow legitimate governments,"[6] conflict diamonds have in the past comprised a notable portion of international trade and export. It is for this reason Djibouti feels that it is our responsibility and the responsibility of the international community to not only hold violators, including sovereign states, corporations, individuals, insurgents and rebels accountable for the mining and exportation of conflict diamonds, but also to uphold international trade standards and ensure that the transportation of conflict diamonds is eliminated before an inflammation of the situation in question. Djibouti feels that conflict diamonds most certainly falls under the auspices of Article 14 under the UN Charter specifically dealing with the "Peaceful adjustment of any situation...which it deems likely to impair the general welfare of friendly relations among nations." The Republic of Djibouti believes that upholding state sovereignty should be a top priority, duly noting that state's violation of human rights is not in accordance with Article I, Section 3 in the United Nations Charter. Djibouti feels that the KPCS is flawed for the following reasons: a lack of enforcement of the scheme's provisions, a lack of economic incentives to follow the provisions, and lack of specificities with regard to a number of definitions and procedures in the KPCS document. Djibouti recommends strengthening the Kimberly Process Certification Scheme [KPCS] with economic incentives and economic penalties with respect to the United Nations Security Council, specifically Chapter VII, Article 41 of the United Nations Charter. Djibouti also recommends that the Economic and Social Council [ECOSOC] take up this serious and trying issue with respect to Chapter X, Article 71 of the UN Charter with due regard especially being paid to the World Trade Organization [WTO] and other NGOs that have the ability to induce compliance with the KPCS protocols. With respect to "the decision of the General Council of the World Trade Organization of 15 May 2003 granting a waiver with respect to the measures taken to implement the Kimberly Process Certification Scheme,"[7] Djibouti feels that this decision by the WTO set a poor example with respect to full and unbiased implementation of KPCS. Regarding the relationship between conflict diamonds and armed conflict, Djibouti feels that the most effective means of eliminating both internal state conflict and transnational terrorist operations is to eliminate the funding of these organizations with respect to blood diamonds by the strengthening of the Kimberley Process as discussed earlier.

III.   Implementation of 2001-2010 International Decade to Roll Back Malaria in Developing Countries, particularly in Africa

The Republic of Djibouti is fully supportive of the initiative to roll back malaria with respect to prevention and treatment of this devastating disease. Djibouti recognizes the massive danger that malaria has on populations, particularly in Africa. In 2000, along with forty three other countries, Djibouti signed the Abuja Declaration of 2000, which amongst other recommendations states the goal of halving the mortality of malaria in Africa by 2010.[8] Djibouti recognizes that fighting malaria is a multi-vectored project, or as WHO has stated on numerous occasions: "Malaria control requires an integrated approach comprising prevention including vector control and treatment with effective antimalarials."[9]

Djibouti feels that the main issue with respect to implantation of eradication of malaria vectors and treatment of those stricken with malaria is the inability of UN agencies and NGOs to successfully coordinate with the countries and regions where malaria is endemic, thereby leading to increased malaria transmission and malaria-related deaths. Malaria is an easily preventable disease that can be easily tamed and eliminated with basic goods such as insecticide impregnated nets and indoor residual spraying (IRS). With the ability to impregnate mosquito nets at the factories as opposed to reapplying insecticide every year to the nets, Djibouti feels that these nets should be heavily subsidized by the states where malaria is endemic or should be given out for free, thereby alleviating the economic and human costs associated with this devastating disease. Djibouti feels that the developed countries, although promising to help with the fight against malaria, has not fully fulfilled their promises with respect to the funding that was asked for and promised by donor nations.

Djibouti agrees with WHO's recommendation with respect to IRS, especially its stance on DDT.[10] IRS would most certainly help with the malaria situation and it is also a relatively cheap way to stop vector transmission of *Plasmodium*. Although Djibouti understands the environmental consequences of using DDT, Djibouti feels that saving human lives is certainly a priority over the small chance of DDT actually being an environmental hazard, which is perfectly in line with WHO guidelines and specifications. Djibouti also feels very strongly that Artenisium derived drugs in conjunction with other anti-malarial drugs is a cheap and effective way to fight malaria when humans are actively infected with the parasite. Djibouti strongly urges the international community to engage in productive, stimulating debate on this issue, leading to a resolution that is acceptable by all Member States of the United Nations, and also wishes to remind the international community that lives are indeed at stake from this grave disease.

CHAPTER FIVE

RULES OF PROCEDURE

Model UN uses a set of modified parliamentary rules to run a committee. This chapter will walk you through the ins and outs of the rules, and show you how to make the highest use of them. There is also a simple chart for you to follow at the end of the chapter outlining what is required for each rule. Be forewarned: these are standard conference regulations. Some conferences use slight modifications of them.

What is committee, exactly?

Committee is where you will actually begin your Model UN experience. You will show up at the conference with all of your materials ready, your position paper written (and already turned in by this point) and yourself dressed appropriately. Your committee might be GA 1st, GA 3rd or a specialized committee like WHO or the Security Council. All of your teammates will be on different committees, but you will all be representing the same country. There will be an opening ceremony, which you are expected to attend. After this, you will be escorted to or told where your committee room is. The committee officially begins when roll is taken. A country can answer in two ways: 'present' or 'present and voting.' If your country is recorded as present, they can abstain during voting procedure. If your country is recorded as present and voting, they CANNOT abstain and MUST vote "yes" or "no" during voting procedure. If you are not sure of your country's position or would like to allow yourself more voting options, go ahead and state that your country is present during roll. For the next few pages, we will assume that we are representing the delegation of Australia.

In committee, a certain set of rules must be used. If you ignore or do not use these rules, you will never be able to master Model UN. Hence, be sure to understand and follow all of them.

After the roll is taken, the chair will ask for motions. At this point, the agenda must be set. Usually you will have researched three or four topics for your committee. However, the order in which these topics will be discussed is up for debate. To motion for adoption of the agenda, say: "The delegation of Australia motions to set the agenda as 3-2-1" (or whichever order you choose). Once the agenda is set, debate will begin on the first topic.

It is imperative that you dress your absolute best on your first day: professionalism is very important to not only the chairs and the Secretariat, but also to your ability to influence others. Think about it: would you listen to someone who looked like he or she had just rolled out of bed? The same applies for hygiene: take a shower! Make sure that you are clean and presentable BEFORE you walk in, not after someone brings it to your attention. By that point, you would have already lost.

How do I make motions in committee?

To make any kind of motion, you must raise your placard (the piece of paper or cardboard with your country's name on it) and wait for the chair to recognize you. Do NOT simply raise your placard and start talking; that is considered very bad form. If you lose your placard, not only can you not be recognized, you cannot vote! Make sure that you keep very careful track of your placard. Otherwise, you won't be recognized.

The correct way to speak your motion is as such:

Step 1: Raise your placard *horizontally* so that the chair can read your country's name. Remember: *horizontal* for motions, *vertical* for voting.

Step 2: Wait for the chair to recognize you. Usually the chair will say, "Delegation of Australia, to what point (or what motion) do you rise?"

Step 3: STAND UP and state your motion as such: "The delegation of Australia motions to…"

Again, make sure you wait for the chair to recognize you. The first rule you should always remember when it comes to committee is "DO NOT MAKE THE CHAIR ANGRY,", so always make sure the chair acknowledges you. The only time that the chair does not recognize you is when you motion for a Point of Order, which we will discuss later.

What is simple majority vs. two-thirds majority?

Most people think they know what a simple majority is; after all, it's called simple, it can't be that hard, right? Unfortunately, it's not that easy. Before committee begins, roll is taken. Delegations can answer that they are either present, or present and voting. Make sure to keep a count of the delegations that are actually in committee, as that will be used by the chair to determine what the majority is. Let's say that there are 50 committees present. Simple majority is NOT 25 delegations: instead, it's 26. Always remember: simple majority is **50% plus 1.** Many motions have failed because delegates have forgotten this simple rule, so don't let that happen to you!

A two-thirds majority is slightly easier. It is what it says: two-thirds of the delegations present must vote for this motion to pass. If math is not your strength, then bring a calculator so that you can always know exactly how many yes votes you need to pass a two-thirds majority.

This rule also applies to voting: however, during voting delegations you can do something called *abstaining*. Abstaining means that the delegation removes itself from voting. That means the count for a simple majority or a two-thirds majority does not include them. For instance, let's say there are 100 delegations, and two delegations vote yes, one votes no, and 97 abstain. That means the resolution passed, 2-1-97.

What is a moderated caucus? What is an unmoderated caucus?

A *caucus* is a break in the formal rules of committee—kind of like a recess. During formal debate, delegations are not allowed to talk; however, they are allowed to pass notes (in larger committees, the management of note passing is the responsibility of a page). During formal debate, only certain motions can be made, and it is considered rude to move about during someone else's speech. A caucus breaks this routine; allowing delegates to move about and talk. There are two kinds of caucuses: a moderated caucus and an unmoderated caucus. Usually, college models do not have moderated caucuses.

A moderated caucus is where the chair allows a less structured debate: the delegations will raise their placard, and the chair will call on them. The called-upon delegation will speak for 30 seconds or so, depending on the chair, and then the chair will call on another delegation. These can be called anywhere from five minutes to 20 minutes. If you are having trouble getting your voice heard, try to motion for one of these. To motion for a moderated caucus, simply say: "The delegation of Australia motions for an X-minute moderated caucus with an X-minute speaker's time," where the first time is the length of the whole moderated caucus and the second time is the time for each speaker to talk.

An unmoderated caucus is where the rules of debate are completely suspended. In fact, most of the time in committee will be spent in unmoderated caucus, so it is important to understand what it is, and what to do during one. Once an unmoderated caucus has been called, delegates are free to move about and talk with each other. However, you are still in committee; this is not the time to trade insults or anything else of a personal nature. You must still act professionally; the chair and his or her associates will be circling the room, listening to what you are doing and taking notes. To call for an unmoderated caucus, say: "The delegation of Australia motions for an X-minute unmoderated caucus" or "The delegation of Australia motions for the suspension of the meeting for the purposes of an X-minute caucus."

What is the speaker's list, and how do I open and close it?

The *speaker's list* is the list of countries who will speak on the topic at hand, in the order stated. It is *imperative* that you stay on the speaker's list as much as possible, even if you do not have much to say. In this way, you are seen more not only by the chair, but also by your fellow delegates.

When session begins, the chair will ask for delegations who wish to be placed on the speaker's list. You are NOT talking about any topic. The first topic that is always discussed is the order of the agenda. Once the order has been determined, the speaker's list is wiped clean and a new speaker's list is taken. This happens every time the topic changes so do not think that just because you are on the speaker's list for this topic you will be on it for the next one.

It is vital to stay on the speaker's list as much as possible. Once the initial speaker's list has been taken, the only way to get back on the speaker's list is to send a note to the chair. My recommendation would be to bring a note with you when you begin to speak; after you have finished speaking, simply drop it on the dais for the chair to read. In this way, you are always on the speaker's list.

The speaker's list is considered open until the committee decides to close it. To close the speaker's list is a simple majority vote. Motion as such: "The Delegation of Australia motions to close the speaker's list." When the speaker's list is closed, no other speakers may be added to the list unless the list is reopened. Use this when it is clear that debate is beginning to wind down; when there are no more speakers left, the committee automatically moves to voting procedure (Chapter Nine).

How do I set the speaker's time?

Why would you want to set the speaker's time, you might ask? What if the speaker's time is 30 seconds and you are speaking next? Or what if someone is about to speak and you do not want them to speak? Then you need to set the time. To set the time, motion: "The delegation of Australia motions to set the speaker's time at X minutes."

Do not use this motion too often; only use it when necessary. Chairs do not like it when time is wasted over whether people speak for two or three minutes. Be careful with your motions.

What kind of vocabulary must I know to sound and act successful?

Dais: This is where the chair and his/her subordinates are (usually an assistant chair, and, occasionally, a page, whose job it is to pass notes in the committee; pages are usually only in larger committees).

Working Paper: This is a committee paper that is in process, and has not been formally introduced to the dais.

Draft Resolution: This is a paper that has been introduced to the floor and has been approved by the chair, but has not been voted on yet.

Dilatory: The chair can rule a motion dilatory if s/he feels that the motion is incorrect or not conducive to debate. It is not desirable for your motions to be dilatory.

Sponsor: A sponsor of a draft resolution is a delegation who either wrote or believes very strongly in what is written in the working paper. Being a sponsor of something means that you absolutely want this working paper to pass; usually 10-15% of the committee is required to sponsor a working paper before the chair looks at it. A sponsor can block friendly amendments added on to the working paper.

Signatory: A signatory may or may not agree with a draft resolution, but is willing to see it go on the floor for further evaluation. A signatory has no power over amendments. These countries are only signing on the working paper; they are not actually writing it or fully endorsing it. Usually a paper needs 10-15% of the committee as signatories before the chair will look at it.

How can I use these rules to my advantage?

Parliamentary rules are set up so that only after careful deliberation is any decision reached. This can be used to your advantage. Let's say, for instance, that you have a working paper on the floor that you have worked really hard to prepare. Let's say that someone is attempting to steal the idea in your paper and they are trying to make it their own. What can you do to stop them? Unfortunately, telling the chair is not an option. However, you can make sure your allies are aware of the situation and attempt to move into voting procedure as quickly as possible. To close debate requires a two-thirds majority, but to close the speaker's list only requires a simple majority. Try to get the speaker's list closed and then attempt to move through the speaker's list as quickly as possible. Finally, if possible, try to stop any kind of caucusing.

On the exact opposite side, what if you need more time? Procedure is your best friend here as well. Try to motion for as many caucuses as possible, moderated or otherwise. Do not motion them all by yourself; seek the help of some of your allies. Try to keep the speaker's list open and the speaker's time as long as possible.

Chapter Review

1. What is a simple majority?

2. If I only have 50 'yes' votes in a 100 person committee, is there any way I can get a resolution to pass? How?

3. What does abstain mean? Why is it important?

4. Why is it important to stay on the speaker's list?

5. I want to delay the committee for long enough to get my working paper on the floor. How would I do that?

6. How do I make a motion?

7. What is the dais?

8. What is the difference between a sponsor and a signatory?

9. What is the difference between a moderated and an unmoderated caucus? How can I use these to get what I want?

10. What is the difference between 'present' and 'present and voting'?

Rules of Procedure Reference Sheet

This is a generic rules reference sheet. Check the background guide for the conference your team is attending to ascertain how that conference runs and also that conference's order of precedence.

Adoption of Agenda: Simple majority.
Set Speaker's Time: 2 for, 2 against; simple majority.
Point of Order: No vote, ONLY errors in formal procedure.
Point of Information: Requested only from speakers during formal debate.
Right of Reply: Only used when your COUNTRY or HEAD OF STATE has been insulted; note to chair about the insult; chair will determine how long you are allowed to speak.
Close Speaker's List: Simple majority.
Table Topic: 2 for, 2 against; 2/3 majority.
Unmoderated Caucus: Simple majority; takes precedence over moderated caucus.
Moderated caucus: Simple majority.
Appeal the chair: 2/3 majority; it is very unwise to use this motion.
Closure of debate: 2 against; 2/3 majority; immediately enter voting procedure.
Withdrawing: ALL sponsors must agree to withdraw.

Table 5.1 Rules of Procedure Reference List

Name of Rule	Debate?	Vote?
Adoption of Agenda	No	Simple
Speaker's Time	2 for/2 against	Simple
Close speaker's list	No	Simple
Table Topic	2 for/2 against	2/3
Unmoderated Caucus	No	Simple
Moderated Caucus	No	Simple
Appeal the Chair	No	2/3
Closure of Debate	2 against	2/3

CHAPTER SIX

HOW TO RUN A COMMITTEE

Now you have the rules of committee. Of course, those rules are worthless if you're sitting in the back doing nothing, right? This chapter will help you gain the confidence necessary to take on anyone and anything.

How can I learn leadership?

Surprisingly, leadership is a skill that can be learned. There are books upon books written on this subject, but here we offer a general overview of what is needed to be an effective leader, or at least to project the appearance of one.

Leadership requires the projection of confidence in oneself. Specifically, you do not have to have faith in yourself. However, it must *appear* that you have confidence in yourself to others. A common maxim that works more often than not is "fake it till you make it." What this means is that even though you may not personally believe in yourself, if you project confidence, people believe in you, and you conversely begin to believe in yourself. At first, it is very difficult. You question yourself in your head over and over again:

- "Do I know what I'm doing?"
- "What if people see through this?"
- "What happens when someone finally calls me out for not knowing what's going on?"

The first rule of thumb: Do not panic! The people you are talking to are just as scared, if not more so, of looking bad, as you are. They are in the exact same boat that you are in, and they are probably having the same doubts as yours. This can be used to your advantage. Again, it is simply a question of *projecting* confidence. By having confidence in yourself, others will see this and lend greater weight to what you are saying. This leads to a snowball effect where more and more people take what you say very seriously, turning you into a star player in the committee.

The best way to learn leadership is to *practice* leadership. Join a club, run for a school office, volunteer for a charity, and above all, interact with people to sharpen your skills. Leadership is not a solitary enterprise: in Model UN, you will realize very quickly that those who attempt to lead alone will simply fail to garner support to pass any resolution in committee and others will ignore them. Leadership in Model UN is usually based upon consensus leadership, where delegates will come together to forge resolutions and move issues that they believe are relevant through debate to voting procedure. Leadership in this case means leadership of many, not a dictatorship of one. Practice consensus leadership before you go into committee; it will most certainly help you.

How can I get people to pay attention to me?

There are a number of different ways to gain the attention, both good and bad, of your peers. You will see at a number of conferences that someone at some point will get on a chair/table and yell for their voting bloc to come to them so that they can plan strategy. This is a terrible idea: people who yell or shout in committee usually do not get results and are seen as bossy and obnoxious.

The delegations that are rude to people at the beginning of the conference will almost guarantee a loss by the end of the conference. Being rude to a delegation might score you quick, cheap victory points with other delegations early, but in the end will sink your ability to effectively work with other delegations. However, on the opposite side of the coin, some delegations might simply be ill-prepared, ill-advised, or flat-out wrong in their policy and/or ideas. This is an excellent opportunity to correct them in a polite and diplomatic manner. Some excellent phrases to use:

"Please allow me to understand what your position is, but you are saying that (reiterate what the delegation said here)…:" this allows other delegations to see that you are polite while allowing the delegate who made the original mistake to repeat or correct it. By repeating the mistake, the delegation further compounds their error, and by correcting it, they acknowledge that they might not have all their facts in order. Either way, you come out ahead.

"I appreciate your idea on this topic and thank you. I was hoping that you would hear my ideas on the issue…:" this allows you to tactfully slip your idea into the discussion without insulting the other delegate.

"That is an interesting way to look at this issue. Have you considered…?" The same idea as above: acknowledge the other person's ideas and then give them yours.

Sometimes, you will not win someone over with logic, coercion or any other means at your disposal. Remember that you do not need every vote to pass a resolution. In such a case, the five minute rule is most effective: if you can't convince someone that the idea in question at least has merit in five minutes, your time can be used more effectively elsewhere. Shake hands with the delegate, thank them for the discussion and move on. Delegates can be time traps; do not let them be.

Teddy Roosevelt said it best: "Speak softly, but carry a big stick." Know your material, be polite and respectful, but make sure that if someone is out of policy or lacks basic knowledge, politely, but firmly, shut them down, showing that you not only have a commanding grasp of the issues, but also that you have the skills required to lead the committee in discussion.

How can I run a caucus?

To get people to caucus with you, find the delegations that would have similar views on the topic. For instance, let us say the topic is desertification and you represent the country of Morocco. It would be logical to begin talking to delegations that are very close to your position on the topic, such as Tunisia, Libya and Algeria. With these delegations working with you, you can expand to countries that take a similar position, but might have slight differences, such as Egypt and Sudan. Then you can continue to expand your voting bloc in this way by slowly, but surely, incorporating additional delegations into your coalition on the topic.

When you begin caucusing and talking to delegations, it is imperative that you fully grasp your topic, any technical information regarding it, and your delegation's position. Remember that other delegations are trying to become the power-brokers of the committee as well and will look for any excuse to call you out on what you do not know. Do not give them the opportunity to do this. Make sure that you have fully brushed up on what you know. If necessary, it is all right to say "I don't know," but it is also imperative that you know where to find the answer to the question, and quickly; otherwise delegations might think that you are not fully prepared.

How can I get my resolution to pass, and conversely, how can I make sure that someone else's does not get passed?

There are a number of procedural methods to give a resolution a better chance of passing. The key to getting a resolution passed is to make sure that the resolution has the appropriate number of votes to pass. If you do not take this point into consideration, you will waste your time. If the resolution can pass, then the following parliamentary tools can be used to force a vote. The first motion that should be made to nudge the committee in the direction of voting is closing the speaker's list, which places a time limit on the committee, because when the speaker's list is exhausted, the committee automatically moves to voting procedure. After this motion, it would be logical to shorten the speaker's time, thereby forcing the speaker's list to move faster. Try to limit caucuses, and if caucuses are still passing committee, attempt to pass the shortest caucuses possible. Make sure to infiltrate the opposition to break them apart before voting procedure so that your faction's resolution will pass. Last but not least, if the committee is moving in the direction of voting, then motion for closure of debate. Usually closure of debate requires a two-thirds majority in conferences. If the votes are there, by all means, motion for closure of debate and vote on the resolutions.

On the opposite side of the spectrum, sometimes it is necessary to force another delegation's resolution to fail. In this case, there are more options present to stall or end a resolution's usefulness. One of the first ways is to simply sabotage the opposition's working paper. This is accomplished by introducing unfriendly amendments to undermine the substance of the working paper. These can be very useful for adding material that is not originally wanted in the original working paper but that also can be used to strip operative clauses out of it. Another effective tactic is as old as history itself: divide and conquer the opposition. Instead of attacking a unified front, pull delegates who are of the periphery to attempt to convince them that the working paper in question is not the most effective one for them. With respect to parliamentary procedure, there are also many ways to delay a vote on the working paper to allow more time to discard it. The most important point is to not allow the debate to end. This requires making sure that a motion for closure of debate fails and that the speaker's list is never exhausted. As discussed in Chapter Five, closure of debate usually requires a two-thirds majority. Therefore, building a minority coalition intent on blocking closure can easily be obtained. It is also imperative to make sure the speaker's list is not closed and that delegates are continuously added to the speaker's list. The best way to do this is to get a small number of delegations to repeatedly place themselves on the speaker's list to keep it from exhausting. Also, it is vital to defeat any motion to close the speaker's list, which requires a simple majority. Although it is difficult to cobble together a coalition to stop closure of the speaker's list, it can be done. Another method to delay the opposition is to push for long caucuses. Instead of 10 or 15 minutes, attempt 20 or 30 minutes as a delaying tactic. Yet another delaying strategy is lengthening the speaker's time as long as possible, requiring a simple majority to extend the speaker's time. All of these strategies are designed to delay and stall the opposition as long as possible and to tire them out, leading them to make tactical errors which can be to the advantage of a delegation, if they are savvy enough.

What is the number one rule in committee?

There is one rule that must be followed in committee at all times: the dais (be it the chair, the director or the assistant director) is always right. Hence, never appeal the chair. If someone else appeals the chair, never vote for it under any circumstances. The chair will take notes of who voted for it, and s/he will not deal with those delegates in the same way again. If the conference you are attending gives out awards, anyone who votes for appealing the chair will almost always not make it on the list of winners. If you need to point of order the chair, be absolutely sure that you are correct. Chairs are human beings and make mistakes; however, they have egos as well. Tread carefully when using points of order. Also, it must be stated that excessive flattery directed towards the chair is almost never a good idea. The chair can and will see right through it, and that will cost you points.

Therefore, how do you deal with a chair or a dais that is simply wrong? First, politely approach the chair during a caucus and point out the error you think they made. If this approach fails, do not try it again. Thank the chair for their time and walk away. Sometimes, the chair will simply not see the error of their ways and if you continue to push the point, they will become angry and simply ignore you. If the first attempt does not work, you no longer have the ability to question the chair: contact your head delegate or your sponsor to talk to the conference staff. At this point, the problem is officially out of your hands. Do not hold a grudge against the chair; it will do you no good whatsoever and will simply harm your future chances. If there is a serious issue, your faculty advisor or your head delegate will bring it up with the committee staff and, if serious enough, the problem will be rectified. If it is not, you will simply have to deal with the chair as is.

CHAPTER SEVEN

PUBLIC SPEAKING

Now we have the rules, and we know how to use them. However, many of you may have a great deal of stage fright and may feel they cannot speak in public. This chapter will take care of that.

Why is it important to learn public speaking?

Public speaking is one of the most important skills to learn in society today. Almost every career will require you, at some point, to give a speech to your colleagues. You may be thinking:

- "I won't take a job like that."
- "I'm too shy; I've never been comfortable in front of people."
- "Speaking in public has always scared me; how in the world can I get over that?"
- "I get cold hands and feel queasy when I'm in front of people."

Hmm. Sounds like a serious problem. Well, here is some news for you. EVERYONE is scared of it! Yes, everyone! But at some point or another, everyone has to do it. Why do you think your teachers make you speak in front of the class at some point in the curriculum? Certainly not because they are bored; actually, they have your best interest at heart. Public speaking is a vital skill to learn in society. Plus, people who are good at public speaking can influence others and change their minds. When have you heard a really good speech and seriously thought about what the speaker was saying? I'm sure you have at some point or another. Now think about this: wouldn't it be nice if someone was thinking that about you?

Many millions of people have died on the various battlefields of history for their beliefs, their cause, and their country. But diplomats and politicians (the decent ones, of course) have managed to avert war. Not with guns, but with words and diplomacy. Does that not sound like something noble to do? Would you not like the ability to stop conflict without starting one? Public speaking can give you that ability.

How can I get over my fear of public speaking?

Public speaking is a skill that everyone should have, yet few people can actually do it effectively. To put your fears at rest, EVERYONE is scared of public speaking, even people who do it for a living. No one is comfortable getting up in front of a group of strangers and talking about anything. It is just that simple. How did those people get over their fear of speaking in public? Practice, practice, practice. That is all there is to it.

Let me tell you about my personal experience with public speaking and Model UN. When I joined Model UN, I was a very shy, introverted person. I was dragged into it by a Model UN sponsor who needed extra bodies for the team's trip to Nationals. I was given a packet of information and told to memorize it, which I dutifully did. Then we got on a plane and headed up to New York.

I stepped into committee for the first time with no experience whatsoever, and no clue what I was doing. I was a sophomore and my partner was a senior who was unhappy being saddled with someone who didn't know what was going on. She wrote me a speech to make on the topic at hand. I remember the speech clearly, word for word. All I had to do was walk up to the podium and read it. It did not sound too difficult at all. The speaker's time was set at 2 minutes. I went to the podium. My hands were clammy and sweaty, my mouth was dry and I froze at the podium in front of 300 people. The only sound that I heard was the gavel dropping at the dais to tell me that my time was up. I had not said a single word the entire time I was at the podium; I was simply too nervous to let anything come out. My partner wanted to kill me.

I was angry at myself for allowing my fear to stand in the way of something I wanted to do. I practiced nonstop for weeks at a time to hone my public speaking skills. By the time our team went to Nationals the next year, I was ready. I went up to that podium with two minutes on the speaker's list, and I gave a great speech on the economic situation in Africa. Not only that, but I also managed to get my resolution passed. After a couple of days of this, I was asked by my entire team to make the team's speech on the General Assembly floor at the United Nations. By my senior year, with my help, my team won an award at Nationals.

Why would I bore you with this story? The reason is the fact that anyone can do public speaking. Some of history's greatest speakers were actually shy and afraid of the crowds, but you would never know that watching them. Remember: EVERYONE is afraid of public speaking. Some people just get used to it. You can get used to it as well.

The first step is to practice in front of a mirror. Yes, that certainly might sound incredibly stupid, but you need to get used to talking. And you need someone to watch you, so why not you? You need to be comfortable hearing the sound of your own voice, and you need to learn how to use your voice as a tool.

After practicing in front of a mirror, try to find a large room, like an auditorium or a theater, and practice ALONE. Try to fill the theater with your voice, but don't strain or push your voice too hard. You should be loud, but not screaming or yelling. Every single person can do this, regardless of size, weight, accent, or otherwise. I have seen the smallest individual figures completely command an audience with their voice alone; it can be done! Again, practice is the key. My recommendation: if you are having trouble projecting your voice, ask a chorus or music teacher for help. They know some tricks that might be able to help you.

Your next step: bring ONE person into the location where you practice (the theater or auditorium) and put them in the very BACK of the room. Practice speaking for two to three minutes. See if the person in the back of the room was able to hear you effectively. If they cannot, do it again, this time more loudly until they can hear you. Do not be afraid of letting go with your voice. Really—everyone can have a powerful voice, including you.

After you have done this for a little while, it is time to bump it up a notch. Bring the team into the theater. Have each person go up to the front to make a speech, and have all the other people on the team wait in the back. The team can either do the same speech, or a different one each. It does not matter. What does matter is that this time around, you are speaking in front of your peers. Have your teammates tell you what you did right, and what you did wrong. Do the same for them. If someone has a stuttering problem, or if they seem too timid on the stage, tell them. How else will they know? On the flip side, make sure to compliment someone if they are speaking well. Again, how else would they know?

Practice this as much as possible. Give speeches in the car. Give speeches at lunch; give speeches to your parents and to the rest of your family. Take every opportunity to hone your skill at public speaking. When you practice, remember: it does not matter WHAT you say. You could be speaking about Mars for all that it matters. The important thing is to SPEAK.

The only way to get comfortable with speaking is to make it not as frightening, and the only way to make it not as frightening is to make it normal, commonplace. The more something is done, the less frightening it is. Many of you, I am sure, are afraid of this. Don't be! Public speaking is a wonderful skill to have! Practice, practice, practice, and it will become so easy you will wonder why you did not do it in the first place!

What is the proper way to speak in public?

Words are very important, yes. But they are not everything when it comes to public speaking. Your posture is also very important. You are a human being: stand up straight! Your mother was right. Slouching is very unprofessional, and makes you look like a slacker. When you stand straight up, you exhibit an air of confidence. When you approach the podium to speak, do it with slow, measured strides. Do not walk fast to the podium, and do not drag your feet. You wish to show that you are in control of yourself at all times. Think about it: imagine someone dragging their feet to the podium, shuffling some papers when they get up there, and mumbling down into the pages. What does that accomplish? What does that say about them? It says that they are incredibly nervous and do not want to be there. You do NOT want to present that kind of picture, do you? Now, let us go over what you should be doing when you are up at the podium:

- Walk upright to the podium; do not run, and do not drag your feet.
- Thank the chair for allowing you to speak; it never hurts to be polite to the chair.
- If you have notes, then place them on the podium. DO NOT READ FROM YOUR NOTES; that gives the appearance that you do not know what you're doing. It is perfectly fine to bring notes; do not bring a fully written speech.
- Do NOT speak down. Speak out to the delegates: you are not speaking to the dais, and you are certainly not speaking to your paper.
- Make eye contact with as many people as possible in the room. Do not stare blankly ahead at one spot the entire time. If you are too shy to make eye contact, that is fine. Instead of looking someone in the eyes, you may look at their forehead or at their nose. This way, you are not looking at their eyes, but they do not know that. It looks like you are looking them directly in the eyes, which is very important.
- Make sure to scan the room while you speak.
- If you wish to inject some emotion into your speech, by all means do so, but keep it sedated. Do not go into hysterics or burst into tears unless the situation truly calls for it. Otherwise you will appear to be superficial.
- When you are finished speaking, make sure to *yield time* to either the chair or to questions if your conference allows yields. If it does not, simply thank the chair and return to your seat.

What is yielding time? When you give the rest of your speaking time to something besides your speech, you are yielding time. In most High School Model UN conferences, you will have three places to yield time: to the chair, to another delegation and to points of information. When you yield time to the chair, you are giving up the rest of your time at the podium, and you simply take your seat. If you yield to another delegation, it is usually wise to tell the chair beforehand that you are doing so before your speech. Usually this is done right when you walk to the podium, where you would say: "I wish to yield my time after my speech to the delegation of X."

The last yield is the most important. A delegation can yield to points of information. This means that the delegation can take questions from the committee. These questions will take up the time allotted for the speech, so it is imperative to keep track of how long you have been speaking so that you will know how much time you have to answer questions. Each question asked has to be only one question: they cannot be strings of questions tied together. It is always wise to yield to questions; otherwise, the other delegates might not be able to express their ideas to you, and you will not be able to get a gauge of what the committee is thinking regarding your ideas. Most college conferences do not allow for yielding of time. Again, check the background guide of the conference that you are attending to ascertain what is and is not allowed.

What do I do with my hands?

Your hands can be doing a great many things, but there are a few things that they should not be doing. One of those things is for your hands to be in your pockets. When your hands are in your pockets, it makes it look as if you are taking a very casual stance, which is not what we want at all. Remember: you are acting as a professional delegate for your country. A state delegate would not look lax; why would you?

It is all right to put your hands on the podium; however, it is not wise to grip the podium like it is a life preserver. Yes, everyone gets nervous. But if you grip the podium very tightly, everyone will know how nervous you are. The more nervous you look the better chance someone will notice and attempt to take advantage of you. This is not what we want at all. If necessary, either rest your hands lightly on the podium, or leave them at your side. You can move them up to the podium and back down again, but try not to do this too frequently.

Again, I cannot stress enough the importance of not putting your hands in your pocket. Make absolutely sure that not only you, but your entire team does not engage in this habit. It will come back to haunt you at some point.

Chapter Review

1. Why is public speaking important at all?

2. How do I go about starting, making and ending my speech?

3. Where can I yield my time?

4. What should I NOT do with my hands, EVER?

CHAPTER EIGHT

RESOLUTIONS

The whole point of a Model UN conference is to pass a resolution favorable to your country's policy. This chapter will walk you through how to write a resolution, what vocabulary to use, and how to make sure the chair accepts your resolution quickly.

What does a resolution do?

A resolution is the main reason for which you are in committee. In theory, a *resolution* is international law once it is passed. However, only the resolutions that are passed by the Security Council are binding on the international community. The resolutions passed by the General Assembly and the other committees are considered to be nonbinding; i.e. they do not hold the force of international law. However, the General Assembly can be considered a sounding board for the world.

Remember that the UN is NOT a world government; it is more of an international forum. The UN only has the ability to enforce Security Council resolutions, and even those are not enforced all the time.

What is the difference between a preambulatory clause and an operative clause?

There are two types of clauses in a resolution: the preambulatory clauses and the operative clauses. The resolution can be looked at as one large sentence, where the preambulatory clauses are the subject or subjects of the sentence and the operative clauses are the action verbs of the sentence. If you look at any number of UN resolutions, you will see that they are all written in the same way. Preambulatory clauses are included in the resolution to set up the history of the issue at hand.

Operative clauses, on the other hand, are there to actually create a solution to the problem or to suggest alternative means of solving the issue at hand.

Preambulatory clauses usually end in –ing, while operative clauses generally end in –s. Also, preambulatory clauses end with commas whereas operative clauses end with semicolons. Table 8.1 shows some samples of preambulatory and operative clauses.

This is an incomplete list; simply remember that most preambulatory clauses end with –ing while most operative clauses are action verbs, usually ending in –s.

Table 8.1 Sample Preambulatory and Operative Clause Verbs

Sample preambulatory clause starting verbs:		Sample operative clause starting verbs:	
Affirming	Having adopted	Accepts	Further reminds
Alarmed by	Having considered	Affirms	Further recom-
Approving	Having considered	Approves	mends
Aware of	further	Authorizes	Further requests
Bearing in mind	Having devoted	Calls	Further resolves
Believing	Having examined	Calls upon	Has resolved
Confident	Having heard	Condemns	Notes
Convinced	Having received	Confirms	Proclaims
Declaring	Having studied	Congratulates	Reaffirms
Deeply concerned	Keeping in mind	Considers	Recommends
Deeply conscious	Noting with deep	Declares accor-	Regrets
Deeply disturbed	concern	dingly	Reminds
Deeply regretting	Noting with approval	Deplores	Requests
Desiring	Noting further	Designates	Solemnly af-
Emphasizing	Noting with regret	Draws the atten-	firms
Expecting	Noting with satisfac-	tion	Strongly con-
Expressing its	tion	Emphasizes	demns
appreciation	Observing	Encourages	Supports
Expressing its	Reaffirming	Endorses	Takes note of
satisfaction	Realizing	Express its ap-	Transmits
Fulfilling	Recalling	preciation	Trusts
Fully alarmed	Recognizing	Express its hope	Urges
Fully aware	Referring	Further invites	
Fully believing	Seeking	Further proc-	
Further deploring	Taking into account	laims	
Further recalling	Taking into consider-		
Guided by	ation		
	Taking note		
	Welcoming		

How do I make sure my resolution makes a difference?

A resolution must initiate some sort of action. To do this, it is imperative that the resolution actually accomplishes an objective, be it directly addressing the problem or making sure that another committee addresses it.

What is an omelet, and why is it a bad thing?

An *omelet* is a term for a resolution that looks pretty on paper, but actually does not accomplish much with respect to the problem. An omelet resolution is one where the resolution contains a large number of preambulatory clauses but only a few operative clauses. The operative clauses usually only call for a committee to be set up or recommends that the problem be sent to another committee.

Just like an omelet in real life, these resolutions are pretty and tasty, but they won't fill you up. In committee, your goal is to NOT write an omelet. The chair frowns on them as they accomplish nothing. It is vital that you understand that resolutions must actually establish something useful; if they do not, you and the committee have wasted your time. Your goal should be to write your operative clauses such that the most important concept or issue is highlighted in the first operative clause. For instance, let us assume that your committee is GA Plen and your country wishes to deal with climate change. The first operative clause will be the clause that accomplishes the most robust realistic result with respect to climate change, like a conference or a new committee. The next operative clauses will support and clarify the first operative clause by giving details on how to implement the new idea.

What are the stages of a resolution?

There are three stages to a resolution: the working paper, the draft resolution and the resolution itself. A *working paper* is a paper that has not been formally introduced to the committee; consider it a rough draft. A working paper usually does not have sponsors or signatories as it is still a work in process. When the drafters of the paper feel it is ready and have the required number of sponsors and signatories, they submit it to the dais for approval. If the dais approves the working paper, the dais will introduce it as a *draft resolution,* which is given a new number for identification purposes.

Once submitted, draft resolutions can only be changed in two ways: friendly and unfriendly amendments (depending on the conference: make sure to check conference rules). A friendly amendment is where all the sponsors agree to change the wording on an operative clause (preambulatory clauses can never be amended, so make sure that you pay close attention to them; once they're in you cannot fix them). No vote is required for a friendly amendment; the dais simply announces the change. An unfriendly amendment is where a number of countries wish to amend an operative clause but they do not have the support of the sponsors of that resolution. An unfriendly amendment undergoes a vote during voting procedure. An unfriendly amendment can change portions of operative clauses, single words in such clauses, or in extreme cases, it can simply strike the entire operative clause. Be mindful of unfriendly amendments; they can easily damage or completely wreck a draft resolution.

A draft resolution becomes a *resolution* when it is passed by the committee during voting procedure. A resolution is the will of the committee, and, in theory, should reflect the majority of the committee's ideas.

Can I see a sample draft resolution?

Below is a draft resolution from a college Model UN conference. As you read it, notice the following technicalities:

1. Commas after the perambulatory clauses, semicolons after the operative clauses;
2. Verbs for perambulatory clauses are in italics, verbs for operative clauses are bolded and underlined;
3. The most important and far-reaching operative clause is first, and each operative clause afterwards is less important or helps to enact the first.

Remember as well that each conference might have different formatting rules, so make sure to read the background guide for your conference.

The General Assembly;

Deeply concerned with the inadequate funding for, and recent decline of official development assistance towards energy investments in the developing world as stated by the Global Network on Energy for Sustainable Development in 2005,

Recognizing the notable contributions of renewable sources of energy to help reduce greenhouse gases and to help address the seriously challenging issues of climate change such as rising sea levels, desertification, frequent and stronger cyclones, reduced fish stocks and extended exposure to contagious diseases,

Recalling the provisions contained in the Plan of Implementation of the World Summit on Sustainable Development (Johannesburg Plan of Implementation) in 2002 concerning energy for sustainable development, including the promotion of renewable energy,

Encouraging initiatives that aim to improve access to reliable, affordable, economically viable, socially acceptable and environmentally sound energy services for sustainable development to realize the achievement of the Millennium Development Goals created by the General Assembly in 2000,

Emphasizing that the World Solar Programme 1996-2005 is aimed at encompassing all forms of new and renewable energy such as solar, hydroelectric, biofuels, wind, geothermal and other forms,

Bearing in mind commitments for developed countries to achieve 0.7% Official Development Assistance, as agreed upon through the Monterrey Consensus in 1992,

1. **Calls for** increased funding from civil society, the private sector and Member States to promote the development, access and utilization of alternate energy resources, thus increasing access to power and increasing the ability to meet the Millennium Development Goals in 2000 to finance international organizations such as the United Nations Environmental Programme specifically the Global Environment Facility and

the Carbon Finance Unit, the United Nations Development Program and the World Bank Energy Program;

2. **Encourages** Member States to utilize already existing grant mechanisms such as the Clean Development Mechanism of the Global Environment Facility, the European Union Energy Initiative and the Organization of Pan-African Non-Petroleum Producers Association;

3. **Encourages** Member States to increase cooperation and coordination at a regional and sub-regional level creating a more enabling environment for the promotion of public-private partnerships by:

   a. Increasing capital to promote sustainable development including infrastructure and alternative energy systems;

   b. The promotion of the accomplishment of agreements that ensure the financial safety of both private and public energy sectors and;

   c. The supervision of the fulfillment of the transfer of energy for developed and developing nations such as the South African and the West African Power Pools began in 2003;

4. **Encourages** Member States to develop and make public energy policies which promote the use of alternative sources of energy to increase transparency.

Prior to becoming a resolution, the working paper would include an alphabetical listing of the sponsors and signatories at the top of the page.

Chapter Review

1.	Why do I need to write or sponsor a resolution?

2.	What is a preambulatory clause?

3.	What is an operative clause?

4.	What is the difference between a preambulatory and an operative clause?

5.	How many sentences are there in a working paper or a draft resolution?

6.	What separates preambulatory clauses from the rest of the document?

7.	What separates operative clauses from the rest of the document?

CHAPTER NINE

VOTING PROCEDURE

Writing a perfect resolution and having the entire committee behind you will not help you a bit if you do not know how to begin and use voting procedure. This chapter will explain the intricacies of voting procedure and how to use this process to your advantage.

So when voting procedure happens, what exactly can't I do?

As discussed in the previous chapters, *voting procedure* is when the committee moves from debate to voting on amendments and draft resolutions. When the motion to close debate passes or when the speaker's list is exhausted, the committee automatically moves to voting procedure. The doors are closed and NO ONE is allowed inside. That means that if your partner leaves to get a beverage, s/he will not be allowed back in until the voting is complete. You may leave, but you may not re-enter.

During voting procedure, there is no talking whatsoever except by the chair and people making motions (of which there are not many). No notes are passed, and even sign language is prohibited. In other words, no communication is allowed between delegations at this point. Chairs are usually very adamant about this, and delegations have been thrown out of committee for such transgressions. Make sure that you do not do anything of this nature! If you get thrown out, you cannot see if your resolution passed or not!

During voting procedure, what exactly happens? In what order does voting occur on resolutions and amendments?

As stated before, during voting procedure the entire committee runs in almost complete silence. There should be no talking, note-passing or anything else of that nature. There is no caucusing and there are no breaks in the procedure.

The order of voting for draft resolutions is based on the order by which the chair has accepted them. This is why it is vital that you get your draft resolution into the dais as quickly as possible; this will give the committee the greatest amount of time to analyze it, and hence discuss it more than any other paper. Voting order for unfriendly amendments is also based on the order of approval by the dais. Friendly amendments, if you will remember from Chapter Eight, are automatically accepted as part of the draft resolution and there is no vote on it.

When voting procedure begins, the first unfriendly amendment (if any) undergoes a vote. This is done by a simple placard vote. The chair will call for all 'Yes' votes, then all 'No' votes, and then any abstentions. If your delegation was recorded as 'Present and Voting' during roll call, you will not be allowed to abstain during this procedure. The chair does pay attention to this, so be careful.

What is a 'roll call vote', and when should I use it?

You may motion for a 'roll call vote' during voting procedure. This requires no votes; it is simply accepted by the dais. During a roll call vote, the chair will randomly pick a starting point on the roll of countries. There are six options that a delegation can use (depending on the conference): 'Yes', 'Yes with Rights', 'No', 'No with Rights', 'Abstain' and 'Pass'. The delegations will be asked in alphabetical order for their vote. If a country passes, that country cannot abstain when the vote comes around to them again. It is imperative to remember this! Therefore, if you promised someone a 'Yes' vote and someone else a 'No' vote and you passed, you cannot abstain to make them both happy; you will have to choose. Be careful on passing.

If a delegation who votes 'No with Rights' wishes to explain their position after the vote for the working paper, usually this is done by a sponsor who was unable to prevent an unfriendly amendment from getting attached to that sponsor's working paper. A delegation who votes 'Yes with Rights' is usually a sponsor who wishes to state, for the record, how much s/he supports the working paper that has been passed. Commonly, chairs find this to be grandstanding and often frown upon it. It is best to remember that voting 'No with Rights' is acceptable, but 'Yes with Rights' usually gets the delegate in trouble.

What is the magic number?

The magic number of a committee is the number of votes required to pass a resolution. Usually, this number is 50% +1 of the committee. It is vital that you get a count of the number of delegations present to determine this number! The chair will not tell you; you must calculate it yourself.

Remember: the magic number can change if delegations abstain. For instance, let us say that there are 50 delegations in the committee. The magic number for this committee would be 26 ($50/2 + 1 = 26$). However, let us say that six delegations have already decided that they will abstain from the voting. The number of ACTIVE delegations voting would then be 44, making the magic number 23. If possible, it is always a good idea to attempt to change no votes to abstentions. Any abstentions will change the magic number to a number more in favor of you. NEVER enter voting procedure until you have confirmed that at least the magic number of delegations will vote in favor of your working paper.

On the flip side, if there is a working paper on the floor that your delegation does not want to pass, make sure that you do not enter voting procedure until you are very sure that your opposition cannot meet the magic number for passing.

What is the nuclear option in voting, and when should I use it?

The nuclear option of voting is division of the question, and should only be used as a last resort when you have nothing left to lose. Division of the question is where an operative clause is actually removed from the resolution and undergoes a separate vote. Usually this is done when every other option has failed. Most delegates do not like division of the question, which is why I call it the nuclear option: you had better be absolutely sure you want to do this when you make the motion.

To motion for division of the question on a working paper, raise your placard. The chair will call on you, and you will say "The Delegation of Australia motions to Divide Operative Clause X from the working paper," where X is the operative clause or clauses in question. You can divide more than one clause at a time from a working paper. You may also make more than one division motion if you would like. The chair will decide in what order to take the motions, usually from most to least damaging.

Once the motion is made, the chair will call for a procedural vote (i.e. no delegation can abstain) on whether to allow for this division. If the vote is 'No', nothing happens and the chair will move on to the next motion on the agenda. If the vote is 'Yes', then the operative clause that was isolated will undergo a separate vote.   For instance, let us say that you like a working paper, except for operative clause number five. You would motion to divide the question and take out operative clause five. If the motion passes, there would be two votes: one on the operative clause by itself and the second on the resolution without operative clause five.

This motion should only be used when you have run out of all other options to make a working paper the way that you want it. It is most definitely a weapon of last resort. If you use this motion too often, you will turn the entire committee against you, including the chair. Be careful with this procedure.

Chapter Review

1. What are the two ways to enter voting procedure?

2. What can I NOT do during voting procedure?

3. Can I pass notes during voting procedure?

4. What is required for a roll call vote?

5. Which item undergoes voting first: amendments or working papers?

6. How do I vote normally in voting procedure? During a roll call vote?

7. Can I abstain after I pass?

8. What is the magic number if I have 75 delegations?

9. What is the nuclear option?

10. Can I divide more than one operative clause out of a working paper?

11. How many times can I divide a working paper?

CHAPTER TEN

RESEARCH

Delegates who do not know their material will fall quickly to the sidelines. This chapter will help you prepare for your conference and show you exactly what you need to know to do well.

Where can I find research sources for my country?

The first stop for any research is your local school library. Most libraries will have some sort of almanac or regional resource for every part of the world. It is vital to know the history of your country, its allies and enemies, and also some specifics; i.e. type of government, head of state, chief exports/imports, etc. If you lack this basic information, another delegate will likely have it and will attempt to make you reveal your ignorance. By knowing this information, you will avoid a trap.

Another excellent spot to go is your advisor. More than likely s/he will have a great deal of knowledge and resources to share with you before conference. The CIA World Factbook is also an excellent place to start your research; it contains basic statistics and bare-bones history of every country in the world.

Where can I find the diplomatic mission for my country?

The diplomatic mission is one of the key sources of information for your country's foreign policy. Most countries have two diplomatic missions, but some only have one. Usually, a country will have a diplomatic mission in its capital city (such as Washington or Ottawa) and it will also have a diplomatic mission to the United Nations in New York City. For Model UN, your best bet would be to check out the diplomatic mission for your country to the United Nations. All of these offices are based in New York City. Most diplomatic missions are more than happy to answer your calls and/or emails, or, in some cases, may send you a great deal of information answering any foreign policy inquiries. Remember, however, that contacting the diplomatic mission and getting material from them will take time. It is recommended that you start your research at least three months prior to the conference so as to allow them time to respond to you and collect the information you might request.

Are there any good websites I can visit? Can't I just use the CIA World Factbook?

There are literally hundreds of websites to visit in order to gain useful information about policy issues and about your country. As stated above, a good starting point is the CIA World Factbook available at: **https://www.cia.gov/library/publications/the-world-factbook/.**

Again, the World Factbook is a good place to *start*; however, it is not the best place to end. It provides only basic information about your country—knowledge that you *must* have—but this is not the only material you will need to successfully compete. Another excellent site for starters is the UN website available at: **http://www.un.org/en/**. There is a great deal of information here on the UN system, and how it interacts with member states. The UN website is also where you will find the official missions to the United Nations for all Member States. If a Member State makes an announcement in any UN committee, it will be on this site.

Another excellent resource is the UN Treaty Series, found at: **http://treaties.un.org/Pages/Home.aspx?lang=en**. Any treaty signed between two or more Member States is registered with the Secretariat and deposited here. Therefore, it would be advisable to search the Treaty Series to see what treaties your country has signed and what your country has not signed so that you are not blindsided in committee. It is always advisable to go to the website of the UN committee you are attempting to represent. These websites are too numerous to list here, but they can be found on the UN website via the main search engine.

If you are a mathematically-oriented person, an excellent site to pull a large number of statistics from is the UN databases, found at: **http://data.un.org/**. These databases are collected by UN agencies on any issue from health statistics to crop yields to carbon dioxide emissions, and more. There are literally hundreds of databases that you can peruse if you want to bolster your speeches with some statistical data. Use it to your advantage.

APPENDIX A

UNITED NATIONS CHARTER

WE THE PEOPLES OF THE UNITED NATIONS DETERMINED to save succeeding generations from the scourge of war, which twice in our lifetime has brought untold sorrow to mankind, and to reaffirm faith in fundamental human rights, in the dignity and worth of the human person, in the equal rights of men and women and of nations large and small, and to establish conditions under which justice and respect for the obligations arising from treaties and other sources of international law can be maintained, and to promote social progress and better standards of life in larger freedom, AND FOR THESE ENDS to practice tolerance and live together in peace with one another as good neighbours, and to unite our strength to maintain international peace and security, and to ensure, by the acceptance of principles and the institution of methods, that armed force shall not be used, save in the common interest, and to employ international machinery for the promotion of the economic and social advancement of all peoples, HAVE RESOLVED TO COMBINE OUR EFFORTS TO ACCOMPLISH THESE AIMS Accordingly, our respective Governments, through representatives assembled in the city of San Francisco, who have exhibited their full powers found to be in good and due form, have agreed to the present Charter of the United Nations and do hereby establish an international organization to be known as the United Nations.

CHAPTER I

PURPOSES AND PRINCIPLES

Article 1

The Purposes of the United Nations are:
1. To maintain international peace and security, and to that end: to take effective collective measures for the prevention and removal of threats to the peace, and for the suppression of acts of aggression or other breaches of the peace, and to bring about by peaceful means, and in conformity with the principles of justice and international law, adjustment or settlement of international disputes or situations which might lead to a breach of the peace;
2. To develop friendly relations among nations based on respect for the principle of equal rights and self-determination of peoples, and to take other appropriate measures to strengthen universal peace;
3. To achieve international co-operation in solving international problems of an economic, social, cultural, or humanitarian character, and in promoting and encouraging respect for human rights and for fundamental freedoms for all without distinction as to race, sex, language, or religion; and
4. To be a centre for harmonizing the actions of nations in the attainment of these common ends.

Article 2

The Organization and its Members, in pursuit of the Purposes stated in Article 1, shall act in accordance with the following Principles.
1. The Organization is based on the principle of the sovereign equality of all its Members.
2. All Members, in order to ensure to all of them the rights and benefits resulting from membership, shall fulfill in good faith the obligations assumed by them in accordance with the present Charter.
3. All Members shall settle their international disputes by peaceful means in such a manner that international peace and security, and justice, are not endangered.
4. All Members shall refrain in their international relations from the threat or use of force against the territorial integrity or political independence of any state, or in any other manner inconsistent with the Purposes of the United Nations.
5. All Members shall give the United Nations every assistance in any action it takes in accordance with the present Charter, and shall refrain from giving assistance to any state against which the United Nations is taking preventive or enforcement action.
6. The Organization shall ensure that states which are not Members of the United Nations act in accordance with these Principles so far as may be necessary for the maintenance of international peace and security.
7. Nothing contained in the present Charter shall authorize the United Nations to intervene in matters which are essentially within the domestic jurisdiction of any state or shall require the Members to submit such matters to settlement under the present Charter; but this principle shall not prejudice the application of enforcement measures under Chapter VII.

CHAPTER II

MEMBERSHIP

Article 3

The original Members of the United Nations shall be the states which, having participated in the United Nations Conference on International Organization at San Francisco, or having previously signed the Declaration by United Nations of 1 January 1942, sign the present Charter and ratify it in accordance with Article 110.

Article 4

1. Membership in the United Nations is open to all other peace-loving states which accept the obligations contained in the present Charter and, in the judgment of the Organization, are able and willing to carry out these obligations.
2. The admission of any such state to membership in the Nations will be effected by a decision of the General Assembly upon the recommendation of the Security Council.

Article 5

A Member of the United Nations against which preventive or enforcement action has been taken by the Security Council may be suspended from the exercise of the rights and privileges of membership by the General Assembly upon the recommendation of the Security Council. The exercise of these rights and privileges may be restored by the Security Council.

Article 6

A Member of the United Nations which has persistently violated the Principles contained in the present Charter may be' expelled from the Organization by the General Assembly upon the recommendation of the Security Council.

CHAPTER III

ORGANS

Article 7

1. There are established as the principal organs of the United Nations: a General Assembly, a Security Council, an Economic and Social Council, a Trusteeship Council, an International Court of Justice, and a Secretariat.
2. Such subsidiary organs as may be found necessary may be established in accordance with the present Charter.

Article 8

The United Nations shall place no restrictions on the eligibility of men and women to participate in any capacity and under conditions of equality in its principal and subsidiary organs.

CHAPTER IV

THE GENERAL ASSEMBLY

Composition

Article 9

1. The General Assembly shall consist of all the Members of the United Nations.
2. Each Member shall have not more than five representatives in the General Assembly.

Functions and Powers

Article 10

The General Assembly may discuss any questions or any matters within the scope of the present Charter or relating to the powers and functions of any organs provided for in the present Charter, and, except as provided in Article 12, may make recommendations to the Members of the United Nations or to the Security Council or to both on any such questions or matters.

Article 11

1. The General Assembly may consider the general principles of co-operation in the maintenance of international peace and security, including the principles governing disarmament and the regulation of armaments, and may make recommendations with regard to such principles to the Members or to the Security Council or to both.

2. The General Assembly may discuss any questions relating to the maintenance of international peace and security brought before it by any Member of the United Nations, or by the Security Council, or by a state which is not a Member of the United Nations in accordance with Article 35, paragraph 2, and, except as provided in Article 12, may make recommendations with regard to any such questions to the state or states concerned or to the Security Council or to both. Any such question on which action is necessary shall be referred to the Security Council by the General Assembly either before or after discussion.

3. The General Assembly may call the attention of the Security Council to situations which are likely to endanger international peace and security.

4. The powers of the General Assembly set forth in this Article shall not limit the general scope of Article 10.

Article 12

1. While the Security Council is exercising in respect of any dispute or situation the functions assigned to it in the present Charter, the General Assembly shall not make any recommendation with regard to that dispute or situation unless the Security Council so requests.

2. The Secretary-General, with the consent of the Security Council, shall notify the General Assembly at each session of any matters relative to the maintenance of international peace and security which are being dealt with by the Security Council and similarly notify the General Assembly, or the Members of the United Nations if the General Assembly is not in session, immediately the Security Council ceases to deal with such matters.

Article 13

1. The General Assembly shall initiate studies and make recommendations for the purpose of:

a. promoting international co-operation in the political field and encouraging the progressive development of international law and its codification;

b. promoting international co-operation in the economic, social, cultural, educational, and health fields, an assisting in the realization of human rights and fundamental freedoms for all without distinction as to race, sex, language, or religion.

2. The further responsibilities, functions and powers of the General Assembly with respect to matters mentioned in paragraph a and b above are set forth in Chapters IX and X.

Article 14

Subject to the provisions of Article 12, the General Assembly may recommend measures for the peaceful adjustment of any situation, regardless of origin, which it deems likely to impair the general welfare or friendly relations among nations, including situations resulting from a violation of the provisions of the present Charter setting forth the Purposes and Principles of the United Nations.

Article 15

1. The General Assembly shall receive and consider annual and special reports from the Security Council; these reports shall include an account of the measures that the Security Council has decided upon or taken to maintain international peace and security.

2. The General Assembly shall receive and consider reports from the other organs of the United Nations.

Article 16

The General Assembly shall perform such functions with respect to the international trusteeship system as are assigned to it under Chapters XII and XIII, including the approval of the trusteeship agreements for areas not designated as strategic.

Article 17

1. The General Assembly shall consider and approve the budget of the Organization.
2. The expenses of the Organization shall be borne by the Members as apportioned by the General Assembly.
3. The Assembly shall consider and approve any financial and budgetary arrangements with specialize agencies referred to in Article 57 and shall examine the administrative budgets of such specialized agencies with a view to making recommendations to the agencies concerned.

Voting

Article 18

1. Each member of the General Assembly shall have one vote.
2. Decisions of the General Assembly on important questions shall be made by a two-thirds majority of the members present and voting. These questions shall include: recommendations with respect to the maintenance of international peace and security, the election of the non-permanent members of the Security Council, the election of the members of the Economic and Social Council, the election of members of the Trusteeship Council in accordance with paragraph 1 of Article 86, the admission of new Members to the United Nations, the suspension of the rights and privileges of membership, the expulsion of Members, questions relating to the operation of the trusteeship system, and budgetary questions.
3. Decisions on other questions, including the determination of additional categories of questions to be decided by a two-thirds majority, shall be made by a majority of the members present and voting.

Article 19

A Member of the United Nations which is in arrears in the payment of its financial contributions to the Organization shall have no vote in the General Assembly if the amount of its arrears equals or exceeds the amount of the contributions due from it for the preceding two full years. The General Assembly may, nevertheless, permit such a Member to vote if it is satisfied that the failure to pay is due to conditions beyond the control of the Member.

Procedure

Article 20

The General Assembly shall meet in regular annual sessions and in such special sessions as occasion may require. Special sessions shall be convoked by the Secretary-General at the request of the Security Council or of a majority of the Members of the United Nations.

Article 21

The General Assembly shall adopt its own rules of procedure. It shall elect its President for each session.

Article 22

The General Assembly may establish such subsidiary organs as it deems necessary for the performance of its functions.

CHAPTER V

THE SECURITY COUNCIL

Composition

Article 23

1. The Security Council shall consist of fifteen Members of the United Nations. The Republic of China, France, the Union of Soviet Socialist Republics, the United Kingdom of Great Britain and Northern Ireland, and the United States of America shall be permanent members of the Security Council. The General Assembly shall elect ten other Members of the United Nations to be non-permanent members of the Security Council, due regard being specially paid, in the first instance to the contribution of Members of the United Nations to the maintenance of international peace and security and to the other purposes of the Organization, and also to equitable geographical distribution.
2. The non-permanent members of the Security Council shall be elected for a term of two years. In the first election of the non- permanent members after the increase of the membership of the Security Council from eleven to fifteen, two of the four additional members shall be chosen for a term of one year. A retiring member shall not be eligible for immediate re-election.
3. Each member of the Security Council shall have one representative.

Functions and Powers
Article 24

1. In order to ensure prompt and effective action by the United Nations, its Members confer on the Security Council primary responsibility for the maintenance of international peace and security, and agree that in carrying out its duties under this responsibility the Security Council acts on their behalf.
2. In discharging these duties the Security Council shall act in accordance with the Purposes and Principles of the United Nations. The specific powers granted to the Security Council for the discharge of these duties are laid down in Chapters VI, VII, VIII, and XII.
3. The Security Council shall submit annual and, when necessary, special reports to the General Assembly for its consideration.

Article 25

The Members of the United Nations agree to accept and carry out the decisions of the Security Council in accordance with the present Charter.

Article 26

In order to promote the establishment and maintenance of international peace and security with the least diversion for armaments of the world's human and economic resources, the Security Council shall be responsible for formulating, with the assistance of the Military Staff Committee referred to in Article 47, plans to be submitted to the Members of the United Nations for the establishment of a system for the regulation of armaments.

Voting

Article 27

1. Each member of the Security Council shall have one vote.
2. Decisions of the Security Council on procedural matters shall be made by an affirmative vote of nine members.
3. Decisions of the Security Council on all other matters shall be made by an affirmative vote of nine members including the concurring votes of the permanent members; provided that, in decisions under Chapter VI, and under paragraph 3 of Article 52, a party to a dispute shall abstain from voting.

Procedure

Article 28

1. The Security Council shall be so organized as to be able to function continuously. Each member of the Security Council shall for this purpose be represented at times at the seat of the Organization.
2. The Security Council shall hold meetings at which each of its members may, if it so desires, be represented by a member of the government or by some other specially designated representative.
3. The Security Council may hold meetings at such places other than the seat of the Organization as in its judgment will best facilitate its work.

Article 29

The Security Council may establish such subsidiary organs as it deems necessary for the performance of its functions.

Article 30

The Security Council shall adopt its own rules of procedure, including the method of selecting its President.

Article 31

Any Member of the United Nations which is not a member of the Security Council may participate, without vote, in the discussion of any question brought before the Security Council whenever the latter considers that the interests of that Member are specially affected.

Article 32

Any Member of the United Nations which is not a member of the Security Council or any state which is not a Member of the United Nations, if it is a party to a dispute under consideration by the Security Council, shall be invited to participate, without vote, in the discussion relating to the dispute. The Security Council shall lay down any such conditions as it deems just for the participation of a state which is not a Member of the United Nations.

CHAPTER VI

PACIFIC SETTLEMENT OF DISPUTES

Article 33

1. The parties to any dispute, the continuance of which is likely to endanger the maintenance of international peace and security, shall, first of all, seek a solution by negotiation, enquiry, mediation, conciliation, arbitration, judicial settlement, resort to regional agencies or arrangements, or other peaceful means of their own choice.
2. The Security Council shall, when it deems necessary, call upon the parties to settle their dispute by such means.

Article 34

The Security Council may investigate any dispute, or any situation which might lead to international friction or give rise to a dispute, in order to determine whether the continuance of the dispute or situation is likely to endanger the maintenance of international peace and security.

Article 35

1. Any Member of the United Nations may bring any dispute, or any situation of the nature referred to in Article 34, to the attention of the Security Council or of the General Assembly.
2. A state which is not a Member of the United Nations may bring to the attention of the Security Council or of the General Assembly any dispute to which it is a party if it accepts in advance, for the purposes of the dispute, the obligations of pacific settlement provided in the present Charter.
3. The proceedings of the General Assembly in respect of matters brought to its attention under this Article will be subject to the provisions of Articles 11 and 12.

Article 36

1. The Security Council may, at any stage of a dispute of the nature referred to in Article 33 or of a situation of like nature, recommend appropriate procedures or methods of adjustment.
2. The Security Council should take into consideration any procedures for the settlement of the dispute which have already been adopted by the parties.
3. In making recommendations under this Article the Security Council should also take into consideration that legal disputes should as a general rule be referred by the parties to the International Court of Justice in accordance with the provisions of the Statute of the Court.

Article 37

1. Should the parties to a dispute of the nature referred to in Article 33 fail to settle it by the means indicated in that Article, they shall refer it to the Security Council.
2. If the Security Council deems that the continuance of the dispute is in fact likely to endanger the maintenance of international peace and security, it shall decide whether to take action under Article 36 or to recommend such terms of settlement as it may consider appropriate.

Article 38

Without prejudice to the provisions of Articles 33 to 37, the Security Council may, if all the parties to any dispute so request, make recommendations to the parties with a view to a pacific settlement of the dispute.

CHAPTER VII

ACTION WITH RESPECT TO THREATS TO THE PEACE, BREACHES OF THE PEACE, AND ACTS OF AGGRESSION

Article 39

The Security Council shall determine the existence of any threat to the peace, breach of the peace, or act of aggression and shall make recommendations, or decide what measures shall be taken in accordance with Articles 41 and 42, to maintain or restore international peace and security.

Article 40

In order to prevent an aggravation of the situation, the Security Council may, before making the recommendations or deciding upon the measures provided for in Article 39, call upon the parties concerned to comply with such provisional measures as it deems necessary or desirable. Such provisional measures shall be without prejudice to the rights, claims, or position of the parties concerned. The Security Council shall duly take account of failure to comply with such provisional measures.

Article 41

The Security Council may decide what measures not involving the use of armed force are to be employed to give effect to its decisions, and it may call upon the Members of the United Nations to apply such measures. These may include complete or partial interruption of economic relations and of rail, sea, air, postal, telegraphic, radio, and other means of communication, and the severance of diplomatic relations.

Article 42

Should the Security Council consider that measures provided for in Article 41 would be inadequate or have proved to be inadequate, it may take such action by air, sea, or land forces as may be necessary to maintain or restore international peace and security. Such action may include demonstrations, blockade, and other operations by air, sea, or land forces of Members of the United Nations.

Article 43

1. All Members of the United Nations, in order to contribute to the maintenance of international peace and security, undertake to make available to the Security Council, on its call and in accordance with a special agreement or agreements, armed forces, assistance, and facilities, including rights of passage, necessary for the purpose of maintaining international peace and security.
2. Such agreement or agreements shall govern the numbers and types of forces, their degree of readiness and general location, and the nature of the facilities and assistance to be provided.
3. The agreement or agreements shall be negotiated as soon as possible on the initiative of the Security Council. They shall be concluded between the Security Council and Members or between the Security Council and groups of Members and shall be subject to ratification by the signatory states in accordance with their respective constitutional processes.

Article 44

When the Security Council has decided to use force it shall, before calling upon a Member not represented on it to provide armed forces in fulfilment of the obligations assumed under Article 43, invite that Member, if the Member so desires, to participate in the decisions of the Security Council concerning the employment of contingents of that Member's armed forces.

Article 45

In order to enable the Nations to take urgent military measures, Members shall hold immediately available national air-force contingents for combined international enforcement action. The strength and degree of readiness of these contingents and plans for their combined action shall be determined, within the limits laid down in the special agreement or agreements referred to in Article 43, by the Security Council with the assistance of the Military Committee.

Article 46

Plans for the application of armed force shall be made by the Security Council with the assistance of the Military Staff Committee.

Article 47

1. There shall be established a Military Staff Committee to advise and assist the Security Council on questions relating to the Security Council's military requirements for the maintenance of international peace and security, the employment and command of forces placed at its disposal, the regulation of armaments, and possible disarmament.
2. The Military Staff Committee shall consist of the Chiefs of Staff of the permanent members of the Security Council or their representatives. Any Member of the United Nations not permanently represented on the Committee shall be invited by the Committee to be associated with it when the efficient discharge of the Committee's responsibilities requires the participation of that Member its work.
3. The Military Staff Committee shall be responsible under the Security Council for the strategic direction of any armed forces paced at the disposal of the Security Council. Questions relating to the command of such forces shall be worked out subsequently.

4. The Military Staff Committee, with the authorization of the Security Council and after consultation with appropriate regional agencies, may establish sub-committees.

Article 48

1. The action required to carry out the decisions of the Security Council for the maintenance of international peace and security shall be taken by all the Members of the United Nations or by some of them, as the Security Council may determine.
2. Such decisions shall be carried out by the Members of the United Nations directly and through their action in the appropriate international agencies of which they are members.

Article 49

The Members of the United Nations shall join in affording mutual assistance in carrying out the measures decided upon by the Security Council.

Article 50

If preventive or enforcement measures against any state are taken by the Security Council, any other state, whether a Member of the United Nations or not, which finds itself confronted with special economic problems arising from the carrying out of those measures shall have the right to consult the Security Council with regard to a solution of those problems.

Article 51

Nothing in the present Charter shall impair the inherent right of individual or collective self-defence if an armed attack occurs against a Member of the United Nations, until the Security Council has taken measures necessary to maintain international peace and security. Measures taken by Members in the exercise of this right of self-defence shall be immediately reported to the Security Council and shall not in any way affect the authority and responsibility of the Security Council under the present Charter to take at any time such action as it deems necessary in order to maintain or restore international peace and security.

Chapter VIII

REGIONAL ARRANGEMENTS

Article 52

1. Nothing in the present Charter precludes the existence of regional arrangements or agencies for dealing with such matters relating to the maintenance of international peace and security as are appropriate for regional action, provided that such arrangements or agencies and their activities are consistent with the Purposes and Principles of the United Nations.
2. The Members of the United Nations entering into such arrangements or constituting such agencies shall make every effort to achieve pacific settlement of local disputes through such regional arrangements or by such regional agencies before referring them to the Security Council.

3. The Security Council shall encourage the development of pacific settlement of local disputes through such regional arrangements or by such regional agencies either on the initiative of the states concerned or by reference from the Security Council.

4. This Article in no way impairs the application of Articles 34 and 35.

Article 53

1. The Security Council shall, where appropriate, utilize such regional arrangements or agencies for enforcement action under its authority. But no enforcement action shall be taken under regional arrangements or by regional agencies without the authorization of the Security Council, with the exception of measures against any enemy state, as defined in paragraph 2 of this Article, provided for pursuant to Article 107 or in regional arrangements directed against renewal of aggressive policy on the part of any such state, until such time as the Organization may, on request of the Governments concerned, be charged with the responsibility for preventing further aggression by such a state.

2. The term enemy state as used in paragraph 1 of this Article applies to any state which during the Second World War has been an enemy of any signatory of the present Charter.

Article 54

The Security Council shall at all times be kept fully informed of activities undertaken or in contemplation under regional arrangements or by regional agencies for the maintenance of international peace and security.

CHAPTER IX

INTERNATIONAL ECONOMIC AND SOCIAL CO-OPERATION

Article 55

With a view to the creation of conditions of stability and well-being which are necessary for peaceful and friendly relations among nations based on respect for the principle of equal rights and self-determination of peoples, the United Nations shall promote:

a. higher standards of living, full employment, and conditions of economic and social progress and development;

b. solutions of international economic, social, health, and related problems; and international cultural and educational co- operation; and

c. universal respect for, and observance of, human rights and fundamental freedoms for all without distinction as to race, sex, language, or religion.

Article 56

All Members pledge themselves to take joint and separate action in co-operation with the Organization for the achievement of the purposes set forth in Article 55.

Article 57

1. The various specialized agencies, established by intergovernmental agreement and having wide international responsibilities, as defined in their basic instruments, in economic, social, cultural, educational, health, and related fields, shall be brought into relationship with the United Nations in accordance with the provisions of Article 63.

2. Such agencies thus brought into relationship with the United Nations are hereinafter referred to as specialized agencies.

Article 58

The Organization shall make recommendations for the co-ordination of the policies and activities of the specialized agencies.

Article 59

The Organization shall, where appropriate, initiate negotiations among the states concerned for the creation of any new specialized agencies required for the accomplishment of the purposes set forth in Article 55.

Article 60

Responsibility for the discharge of the functions of the Organization set forth in this Chapter shall be vested in the General Assembly and, under the authority of the General Assembly, in the Economic and Social Council, which shall have for this purpose the powers set forth in Chapter X.

CHAPTER X

THE ECONOMIC AND SOCIAL COUNCIL

Composition

Article 61

1. The Economic and Social Council shall consist of fifty-four Members of the United Nations elected by the General Assembly.
2. Subject to the provisions of paragraph 3, eighteen members of the Economic and Social Council shall be elected each year for a term of three years. A retiring member shall be eligible for immediate re-election.
3. At the first election after the increase in the membership of the Economic and Social Council from twenty-seven to fifty-four members, in addition to the members elected in place of the nine members whose term of office expires at the end of that year, twenty-seven additional members shall be elected. Of these twenty-seven additional members, the term of office of nine members so elected shall expire at the end of one year, and of nine other members at the end of two years, in accordance with arrangements made by the General Assembly.
4. Each member of the Economic and Social Council shall have one representative.

Functions and Powers

Article 62

1. The Economic and Social Council may make or initiate studies and reports with respect to international economic, social, cultural, educational, health, and related matters and may make recommendations with respect to any such matters to the General Assembly, to the Members of the United Nations, and to the specialized agencies concerned.

2. It may make recommendations for the purpose of promoting respect for, and observance of, human rights and fundamental freedoms for all.
3. It may prepare draft conventions for submission to the General Assembly, with respect to matters falling within its competence.
4. It may call, in accordance with the rules prescribed by the United Nations, international conferences on matters falling within its competence.

Article 63

1. The Economic and Social Council may enter into agreements with any of the agencies referred to in Article 57, defining the terms on which the agency concerned shall be brought into relationship with the United Nations. Such agreements shall be subject to approval by the General Assembly.
2. It may co-ordinate the activities of the specialized agencies through consultation with and recommendations to such agencies and through recommendations to the General Assembly and to the Members of the United Nations.

Article 64

1. The Economic and Social Council may take appropriate steps to obtain regular reports from the specialized agencies. It may make arrangements with the Members of the United Nations and with the specialized agencies to obtain reports on the steps taken to give effect to its own recommendations and to recommendations on matters falling within its competence made by the General Assembly.
2. It may communicate its observations on these reports to the General Assembly.

Article 65

The Economic and Social Council may furnish information to the Security Council and shall assist the Security Council upon its request.

Article 66

1. The Economic and Social Council shall perform such functions as fall within its competence in connexion with the carrying out of the recommendations of the General Assembly.
2. It may, with the approval of the General Assembly, perform services at the request of Members of the United Nations and at the request of specialized agencies.
3. It shall perform such other functions as are specified elsewhere in the present Charter or as may be assigned to it by the General Assembly.

Voting

Article 67

1. Each member of the Economic and Social Council shall have one vote.
2. Decisions of the Economic and Social Council shall be made by a majority of the members present and voting.

Procedure

Article 68

The Economic and Social Council shall set up commissions in economic and social fields and for the promotion of human rights, and such other commissions as may be required for the performance of its functions.

Article 69

The Economic and Social Council shall invite any Member of the United Nations to participate, without vote, in its deliberations on any matter of particular concern to that Member.

Article 70

The Economic and Social Council may make arrangements for representatives of the specialized agencies to participate, without vote, in its deliberations and in those of the commissions established by it, and for its representatives to participate in the deliberations of the specialized agencies.

Article 71

The Economic and Social Council may make suitable arrangements for consultation with non-governmental organizations which are concerned with matters within its competence. Such arrangements may be made with international organizations and, where appropriate, with national organizations after consultation with the Member of the United Nations concerned.

Article 72

1. The Economic and Social Council shall adopt its own rules of procedure, including the method of selecting its President.
2. The Economic and Social Council shall meet as required in accordance with its rules, which shall include provision for the convening of meetings on the request of a majority of its members.

CHAPTER XI

DECLARATION REGARDING NON-SELF-GOVERNING TERRITORIES

Article 73

Members of the United Nations which have or assume responsibilities for the administration of territories whose peoples have not yet attained a full measure of self-government recognize the principle that the interests of the inhabitants of these territories are paramount, and accept as a sacred trust the obligation to promote to the utmost, within the system of international peace and security established by the present Charter, the well-being of the inhabitants of these territories, and, to this end:
a. to ensure, with due respect for the culture of the peoples concerned, their political, economic, social, and educational advancement, their just treatment, and their protection against abuses;

b. to develop self-government, to take due account of the political aspirations of the peoples, and to assist them in the progressive development of their free political institutions, according to the particular circumstances of each territory and its peoples and their varying stages of advancement;

c. to further international peace and security;

d. to promote constructive measures of development, to encourage research, and to co-operate with one another and, when and where appropriate, with specialized international bodies with a view to the practical achievement of the social, economic, and scientific purposes set forth in this Article; and

e. to transmit regularly to the Secretary-General for information purposes, subject to such limitation as security and constitutional considerations may require, statistical and other information of a technical nature relating to economic, social, and educational conditions in the territories for which they are respectively responsible other than those territories to which Chapters XII and XIII apply.

Article 74

Members of the United Nations also agree that their policy in respect of the territories to which this Chapter applies, no less than in respect of their metropolitan areas, must be based on the general principle of good-neighbourliness, due account being taken of the interests and well-being of the rest of the world, in social, economic, and commercial matters.

CHAPTER XII

INTERNATIONAL TRUSTEESHIP SYSTEM

Article 75

The United Nations shall establish under its authority an international trusteeship system for the administration and supervision of such territories as may be placed thereunder by subsequent individual agreements. These territories are hereinafter referred to as trust territories.

Article 76

The basic objectives of the trusteeship system, in accordance with the Purposes of the United Nations laid down in Article 1 of the present Charter, shall be:

a. to further international peace and security;

b. to promote the political, economic, social, and educational advancement of the inhabitants of the trust territories, and their progressive development towards self-government or independence as may be appropriate to the particular circumstances of each territory and its peoples and the freely expressed wishes of the peoples concerned, and as may be provided by the terms of each trusteeship agreement;

c. to encourage respect for human rights and for fundamental freedoms for all without distinction as to race, sex, language, or religion, and to encourage recognition of the interdependence of the peoples of the world; and

d. to ensure equal treatment in social, economic, and commercial matters for all Members of the United Nations and their nationals, and also equal treatment for the latter in the administration of justice, without prejudice to the attainment of the foregoing objectives and subject to the provisions of Article 80.

Article 77

1. The trusteeship system shall apply to such territories in the following categories as may be placed thereunder by means of trusteeship agreements:
a. territories now held under mandate;
b. territories which may be detached from enemy states as a result of the Second World War; and
c. territories voluntarily placed under the system by states responsible for their administration.
2. It will be a matter for subsequent agreement as to which territories in the foregoing categories will be brought under the trustee- ship system and upon what terms.

Article 78

The trusteeship system shall not apply to territories which have become Members of the United Nations, relationship among which shall be based on respect for the principle of sovereign equality.

Article 79

The terms of trusteeship for each territory to be placed under the trusteeship system, including any alteration or amendment, shall be agreed upon by the states directly concerned, including the mandatory power in the case of territories held under mandate by a Member of the United Nations, and shall be approved as provided for in Articles 83 and 85.

Article 80

1. Except as may be agreed upon in individual trusteeship agreements, made under Articles 77, 79, and 81, placing each territory under the trusteeship system, and until such agreements have been concluded, nothing in this Chapter shall be construed in or of itself to alter in any manner the rights whatsoever of any states or any peoples or the terms of existing international instruments to which Members of the United Nations may respectively be parties.
2. Paragraph 1 of this Article shall not be interpreted as giving grounds for delay or postponement of the negotiation and conclusion of agreements for placing mandated and other territories under the trusteeship system as provided for in Article 77.

Article 81

The trusteeship agreement shall in each case include the terms under which the trust territory will be administered and designate the authority which will exercise the administration of the trust territory. Such authority, hereinafter called the administering authority, may be one or more states or the Organization itself.

Article 82

There may be designated, in any trusteeship agreement, a strategic area or areas which may include part or all of the trust territory to which the agreement applies, without prejudice to any special agreement or agreements made under Article 43.

Article 83

1. All functions of the United Nations relating to strategic areas, including the approval of the terms of the trusteeship agreements and of their alteration or amendment, shall be exercised by the Security Council.
2. The basic objectives set forth in Article 76 shall be applicable to the people of each strategic area.
3. The Security Council shall, subject to the provisions of the trusteeship agreements and without prejudice to security considerations, avail itself of the assistance of the Trusteeship Council to perform those functions of the United Nations under the trusteeship system relating to political, economic, social, and educational matters in the strategic areas.

Article 84

It shall be the duty of the administering authority to ensure that the trust territory shall play its part in the maintenance of international peace and security. To this end the administering authority may make use of volunteer forces, facilities, and assistance from the trust territory in carrying out the obligations towards the Security Council undertaken in this regard by the administering authority, as well as for local defence and the maintenance of law and order within the trust territory.

Article 85

1. The functions of the United Nations with regard to trusteeship agreements for all areas not designated as strategic, including the approval of the terms of the trusteeship agreements and of their alteration or amendment, shall be exercised by the General Assembly.
2. The Trusteeship Council, operating under the authority of the General Assembly, shall assist the General Assembly in carrying out these functions.

CHAPTER XIII

THE TRUSTEESHIP COUNCIL

Composition

Article 86

1. The Trusteeship Council shall consist of the following Members of the United Nations:
a. those Members administering trust territories;
b. such of those Members mentioned by name in Article 23 as are not administering trust territories; and
c. as many other Members elected for three-year terms by the General Assembly as may be necessary to ensure that the total number of members of the Trusteeship Council is equally divided between those Members of the United Nations which administer trust territories and those which do not.
2. Each member of the Trusteeship Council shall designate one specially qualified person to represent it therein.

Functions and Powers

Article 87

The General Assembly and, under its authority, the Trusteeship Council, in carrying out their functions, may:
a. consider reports submitted by the administering authority;
b. accept petitions and examine them in consultation with the administering authority;
c. provide for periodic visits to the respective trust territories at times agreed upon with the administering authority; and
d. take these and other actions in conformity with the terms of the trusteeship agreements.

Article 88

The Trusteeship Council shall formulate a questionnaire on the political, economic, social, and educational advancement of the inhabitants of each trust territory, and the administering authority for each trust territory within the competence of the General Assembly shall make an annual report to the General Assembly upon the basis of such questionnaire.

Voting

Article 89

1. Each member of the Trusteeship Council shall have one vote.
2. Decisions of the Trusteeship Council shall be made by a majority of the members present and voting.

Procedure

Article 90

1. The Trusteeship Council shall adopt its own rules of procedure, including the method of selecting its President.
2. The Trusteeship Council shall meet as required in accordance with its rules, which shall include provision for the convening of meetings on the request of a majority of its members.

Article 91

The Trusteeship Council shall, when appropriate, avail itself of the assistance of the Economic and Social Council and of the specialized agencies in regard to matters with which they are respectively concerned.

CHAPTER XIV

THE INTERNATIONAL COURT OF JUSTICE

Article 92

The International Court of Justice shall be the principal judicial organ of the United Nations. It shall function in accordance with the annexed Statute, which is based upon the

Statute of the Permanent Court of International Justice and forms an integral part of the present Charter.

Article 93

1. All Members of the United Nations are facto parties to the Statute of the International Court of Justice.
2. A state which is not of the United Nations may become a party to the Statute of the International Court of Justice on to be determined in each case by the General Assembly upon the recommendation of the Security Council.

Article 94

1. Each Member of the United Nations undertakes to comply with the decision of the International Court of Justice in any case to which it is a party.
2. If any party to a case fails to perform the obligations incumbent upon it under a judgment rendered by the Court, the other party may have recourse to the Security Council, which may, if it deems necessary, make recommendations or decide upon measures to be taken to give to the judgment.

Article 95

Nothing in the present Charter shall prevent Members of the United Nations from entrusting the solution of their differences to other tribunals by virtue of agreements already in existence or which may be concluded in the future.

Article 96

1. The General Assembly or the Security Council may request the International Court of Justice to give an advisory opinion on any legal question.
2. Other organs of the United Nations and specialized agencies, which may at any time be so authorized by the General Assembly, may also request advisory opinions of the Court on legal questions arising within the scope of their activities.

CHAPTER XV

THE SECRETARIAT

Article 97

The Secretariat shall comprise a Secretary-General and such staff as the Organization may require. The Secretary-General shall be appointed by the General Assembly upon the recommendation of the Security Council. He shall be the chief administrative officer of the Organization.

Article 98

The Secretary-General shall act in that capacity in all meetings of the General Assembly, of the Security Council, of the Economic and Social Council, and of the Trusteeship Council, and shall perform such other functions as are entrusted to him by these organs. The Secretary-General shall make an annual report to the General Assembly on the work of the Organization.

Article 99

The Secretary-General may bring to the attention of the Security Council any matter which in his opinion may threaten the maintenance of international peace and security.

Article 100

1. In the performance of their duties the Secretary-General and the staff shall not seek or receive instructions from any government or from any other authority external to the Organization. They shall refrain from any action which might reflect on their position as international officials responsible only to the Organization.
2. Each Member of the United Nations undertakes to respect the exclusively international character of the responsibilities of the Secretary-General and the staff and not to seek to influence them in the discharge of their responsibilities.

Article 101

1. The staff shall be appointed by the Secretary-General under regulations established by the General Assembly.
2. Appropriate staffs shall be permanently assigned to the Economic and Social Council, the Trusteeship Council, and, as required, to other organs of the United Nations. These staffs shall form a part of the Secretariat.
3. The paramount consideration in the employment of the staff and in the determination of the conditions of service shall be the necessity of securing the highest standards of efficiency, competence, and integrity. Due regard shall be paid to the importance of recruiting the staff on as wide a geographical basis as possible.

CHAPTER XVI

MISCELLANEOUS PROVISIONS

Article 102

1. Every treaty and every international agreement entered into by any Member of the United Nations after the present Charter comes into force shall as soon as possible be registered with the Secretariat and published by it.
2. No party to any such treaty or international agreement which has not been registered in accordance with the provisions of paragraph I of this Article may invoke that treaty or agreement before any organ of the United Nations.

Article 103

In the event of a conflict between the obligations of the Members of the United Nations under the present Charter and their obligations under any other international agreement, their obligations under the present Charter shall prevail.

Article 104

The Organization shall enjoy in the territory of each of its Members such legal capacity as may be necessary for the exercise of its functions and the fulfilment of its purposes.

Article 105

1. The Organization shall enjoy in the territory of each of its Members such privileges and immunities as are necessary for the fulfilment of its purposes.
2. Representatives of the Members of the United Nations and officials of the Organization shall similarly enjoy such privileges and immunities as are necessary for the independent exercise of their functions in connexion with the Organization.
3. The General Assembly may make recommendations with a view to determining the details of the application of paragraphs 1 and 2 of this Article or may propose conventions to the Members of the United Nations for this purpose.

CHAPTER XVII

TRANSITIONAL SECURITY ARRANGEMENTS

Article 106

Pending the coming into force of such special agreements referred to in Article 43 as in the opinion of the Security Council enable it to begin the exercise of its responsibilities under Article 42, the parties to the Four-Nation Declaration, signed at Moscow, 30 October 1943, and France, shall, in accordance with the provisions of paragraph 5 of that Declaration, consult with one another and as occasion requires with other Members of the United Nations with a view to such joint action on behalf of the Organization as may be necessary for the purpose of maintaining international peace and security.

Article 107

Nothing in the present Charter shall invalidate or preclude action, in relation to any state which during the Second World War has been an enemy of any signatory to the present Charter, taken or authorized as a result of that war by the Governments having responsibility for such action.

CHAPTER XVIII

AMENDMENTS

Article 108

Amendments to the present Charter shall come into force for all Members of the United Nations when they have been adopted by a vote of two thirds of the members of the General Assembly and ratified in accordance with their respective constitutional processes by two thirds of the Members of the United Nations, including all the permanent members of the Security Council.

Article 109

1. A General Conference of the Members of the United Nations for the purpose of reviewing the present Charter may be held at a date and place to be fixed by a two-thirds vote of the members of the General Assembly and by a vote of any nine members of the Security Council. Each Member of the United Nations shall have one vote in the conference.

2. Any alteration of the present Charter recommended by a two-thirds vote of the conference shall take effect when ratified in accordance with their respective constitutional processes by two thirds of the Members of the United Nations including the permanent members of the Security Council.

3. If such a conference has not been held before the tenth annual session of the General Assembly following the coming into force of the present Charter, the proposal to call such a conference shall be placed on the agenda of that session of the General Assembly, and the conference shall be held if so decided by a majority vote of the members of the General Assembly and by a vote of any seven members of the Security Council.

CHAPTER XIX

RATIFICATION AND SIGNATURE

Article 110

1. The present Charter shall be ratified by the signatory states in accordance with their respective constitutional processes.

2. The shall be deposited with the Government of the Unite States of America, which shall notify all the signatory states of each deposit as well as the Secretary-General of the Organization when he has been appointed.

3. The present Charter shall come into force upon the deposit of by the Republic of China, France, the Union of Soviet Socialist Republics, the United Kingdom of Great Britain and Northern Ireland, and the United States of America, and by a majority of the other signatory states. A protocol of the deposited shall thereupon be drawn up by the Government of the United States of America which shall communicate copies thereof to all the signatory states.

4. The states signatory to the present Charter which ratify it after it has come into force will become original Members of the United Nations on the date of the deposit of their respective ratifications.

Article 111

The present Charter, of which the Chinese, French, Russian, English, and Spanish texts are equally authentic, shall remain deposited in the archives of the Government of the United States of America. Duly certified copies thereof shall be transmitted by that Government to the Governments of the other signatory states.

IN FAITH WHEREOF the representatives of the Governments of the United Nations have signed the present Charter.

DONE at the city of San Francisco the twenty-sixth day of June, one thousand nine hundred and forty-five.

APPENDIX B

INTERNATIONAL COURT OF JUSTICE STATUTE

Article 1

The International Court of Justice established by the Charter of the United Nations as the principal judicial organ of the United Nations shall be constituted and shall function in accordance with the provisions of the present Statute.

CHAPTER I - ORGANIZATION OF THE COURT

Article 2

The Court shall be composed of a body of independent judges, elected regardless of their nationality from among persons of high moral character, who possess the qualifications required in their respective countries for appointment to the highest judicial offices, or are jurisconsults of recognized competence in international law.

Article 3

1. The Court shall consist of fifteen members, no two of whom may be nationals of the same state.
2. A person who for the purposes of membership in the Court could be regarded as a national of more than one state shall be deemed to be a national of the one in which he ordinarily exercises civil and political rights.

Article 4

1. The members of the Court shall be elected by the General Assembly and by the Security Council from a list of persons nominated by the national groups in the Permanent Court of Arbitration, in accordance with the following provisions.
2. In the case of Members of the United Nations not represented in the Permanent Court of Arbitration, candidates shall be nominated by national groups appointed for this purpose by their governments under the same conditions as those prescribed for members of the Permanent Court of Arbitration by Article 44 of the Convention of The Hague of 1907 for the pacific settlement of international disputes.
3. The conditions under which a state which is a party to the present Statute but is not a Member of the United Nations may participate in electing the members of the Court shall, in the absence of a special agreement, be laid down by the General Assembly upon recommendation of the Security Council.

Article 5

1. At least three months before the date of the election, the Secretary-General of the United Nations shall address a written request to the members of the Permanent Court of Arbitration belonging to the states which are parties to the present Statute, and to the members of the national groups appointed under Article 4, paragraph 2, inviting them to undertake, within a given time, by national groups, the nomination of persons in a position to accept the duties of a member of the Court.
2. No group may nominate more than four persons, not more than two of whom shall be of their own nationality. In no case may the number of candidates nominated by a group be more than double the number of seats to be filled.

Article 6

Before making these nominations, each national group is recommended to consult its highest court of justice, its legal faculties and schools of law, and its national academies and national sections of international academies devoted to the study of law.

Article 7

1. The Secretary-General shall prepare a list in alphabetical order of all the persons thus nominated. Save as provided in Article 12, paragraph 2, these shall be the only persons eligible.
2. The Secretary-General shall submit this list to the General Assembly and to the Security Council.

Article 8

The General Assembly and the Security Council shall proceed independently of one another to elect the members of the Court.

Article 9

At every election, the electors shall bear in mind not only that the persons to be elected should individually possess the qualifications required, but also that in the body as a whole the representation of the main forms of civilization and of the principal legal systems of the world should be assured.

Article 10

1. Those candidates who obtain an absolute majority of votes in the General Assembly and in the Security Council shall be considered as elected.
2. Any vote of the Security Council, whether for the election of judges or for the appointment of members of the conference envisaged in Article 12, shall be taken without any distinction between permanent and non-permanent members of the Security Council.
3. In the event of more than one national of the same state obtaining an absolute majority of the votes both of the General Assembly and of the Security Council, the eldest of these only shall be considered as elected.

Article 11

If, after the first meeting held for the purpose of the election, one or more seats remain to be filled, a second and, if necessary, a third meeting shall take place.

Article 12

1. If, after the third meeting, one or more seats still remain unfilled, a joint conference consisting of six members, three appointed by the General Assembly and three by the Security Council, may be formed at any time at the request of either the General Assembly or the Security Council, for the purpose of choosing by the vote of an absolute majority one name for each seat still vacant, to submit to the General Assembly and the Security Council for their respective acceptance.
2. If the joint conference is unanimously agreed upon any person who fulfills the required conditions, he may be included in its list, even though he was not included in the list of nominations referred to in Article 7.
3. If the joint conference is satisfied that it will not be successful in procuring an election, those members of the Court who have already been elected shall, within a period to be fixed by the Security Council, proceed to fill the vacant seats by selection from among those candidates who have obtained votes either in the General Assembly or in the Security Council.
4. In the event of an equality of votes among the judges, the eldest judge shall have a casting vote.

Article 13

1. The members of the Court shall be elected for nine years and may be re-elected; provided, however, that of the judges elected at the first election, the terms of five judges shall expire at the end of three years and the terms of five more judges shall expire at the end of six years.
2. The judges whose terms are to expire at the end of the above-mentioned initial periods of three and six years shall be chosen by lot to be drawn by the Secretary-General immediately after the first election has been completed.
3. The members of the Court shall continue to discharge their duties until their places have been filled. Though replaced, they shall finish any cases which they may have begun.
4. In the case of the resignation of a member of the Court, the resignation shall be addressed to the President of the Court for transmission to the Secretary-General. This last notification makes the place vacant.

Article 14

Vacancies shall be filled by the same method as that laid down for the first election, subject to the following provision: the Secretary-General shall, within one month of the occurrence of the vacancy, proceed to issue the invitations provided for in Article 5, and the date of the election shall be fixed by the Security Council.

Article 15

A member of the Court elected to replace a member whose term of office has not expired shall hold office for the remainder of his predecessor's term.

Article 16

1. No member of the Court may exercise any political or administrative function, or engage in any other occupation of a professional nature.
2. Any doubt on this point shall be settled by the decision of the Court.

Article 17

1. No member of the Court may act as agent, counsel, or advocate in any case.
2. No member may participate in the decision of any case in which he has previously taken part as agent, counsel, or advocate for one of the parties, or as a member of a national or international court, or of a commission of enquiry, or in any other capacity.
3. Any doubt on this point shall be settled by the decision of the Court.

Article 18

1. No member of the Court can be dismissed unless, in the unanimous opinion of the other members, he has ceased to fulfill the required conditions.
2. Formal notification thereof shall be made to the Secretary-General by the Registrar.
3. This notification makes the place vacant.

Article 19

The members of the Court, when engaged on the business of the Court, shall enjoy diplomatic privileges and immunities.

Article 20

Every member of the Court shall, before taking up his duties, make a solemn declaration in open court that he will exercise his powers impartially and conscientiously.

Article 21

1. The Court shall elect its President and Vice-President for three years; they may be re-elected.
2. The Court shall appoint its Registrar and may provide for the appointment of such other officers as may be necessary.

Article 22

1. The seat of the Court shall be established at The Hague. This, however, shall not prevent the Court from sitting and exercising its functions elsewhere whenever the Court considers it desirable.
2. The President and the Registrar shall reside at the seat of the Court.

Article 23

1. The Court shall remain permanently in session, except during the judicial vacations, the dates and duration of which shall be fixed by the Court.
2. Members of the Court are entitled to periodic leave, the dates and duration of which shall be fixed by the Court, having in mind the distance between The Hague and the home of each judge.

3. Members of the Court shall be bound, unless they are on leave or prevented from attending by illness or other serious reasons duly explained to the President, to hold themselves permanently at the disposal of the Court.

Article 24

1. If, for some special reason, a member of the Court considers that he should not take part in the decision of a particular case, he shall so inform the President.
2. If the President considers that for some special reason one of the members of the Court should not sit in a particular case, he shall give him notice accordingly.
3. If in any such case the member Court and the President disagree, the matter shall be settled by the decision of the Court.

Article 25

1. The full Court shall sit except when it is expressly provided otherwise in the present Statute.
2. Subject to the condition that the number of judges available to constitute the Court is not thereby reduced below eleven, the Rules of the Court may provide for allowing one or more judges, according to circumstances and in rotation, to be dispensed from sitting.
3. A quorum of nine judges shall suffice to constitute the Court.

Article 26

1. The Court may from time to time form one or more chambers, composed of three or more judges as the Court may determine, for dealing with particular categories of cases; for example, labour cases and cases relating to transit and communications.
2. The Court may at any time form a chamber for dealing with a particular case. The number of judges to constitute such a chamber shall be determined by the Court with the approval of the parties.
3. Cases shall be heard and determined by the chambers provided for in this article if the parties so request.

Article 27

A judgment given by any of the chambers provided for in Articles 26 and 29 shall be considered as rendered by the Court.

Article 28

The chambers provided for in Articles 26 and 29 may, with the consent of the parties, sit and exercise their functions elsewhere than at The Hague.

Article 29

With a view to the speedy dispatch of business, the Court shall form annually a chamber composed of five judges which, at the request of the parties, may hear and determine cases by summary procedure. In addition, two judges shall be selected for the purpose of replacing judges who find it impossible to sit.

Article 30

1. The Court shall frame rules for carrying out its functions. In particular, it shall lay down rules of procedure.
2. The Rules of the Court may provide for assessors to sit with the Court or with any of its chambers, without the right to vote.

Article 31

1. Judges of the nationality of each of the parties shall retain their right to sit in the case before the Court.
2. If the Court includes upon the Bench a judge of the nationality of one of the parties, any other party may choose a person to sit as judge. Such person shall be chosen prefera-bly from among those persons who have been nominated as candidates as provided in Articles 4 and 5.
3. If the Court includes upon the Bench no judge of the nationality of the parties, each of these parties may proceed to choose a judge as provided in paragraph 2 of this Article.
4. The provisions of this Article shall apply to the case of Articles 26 and 29. In such cases, the President shall request one or, if necessary, two of the members of the Court forming the chamber to give place to the members of the Court of the nationality of the parties concerned, and, failing such, or if they are unable to be present, to the judges spe-cially chosen by the parties.
5. Should there be several parties in the same interest, they shall, for the purpose of the preceding provisions, be reckoned as one party only. Any doubt upon this point shall be settled by the decision of the Court.
6. Judges chosen as laid down in paragraphs 2, 3, and 4 of this Article shall fulfill the conditions required by Articles 2, 17 (paragraph 2), 20, and 24 of the present Statute. They shall take part in the decision on terms of complete equality with their colleagues.

Article 32

1. Each member of the Court shall receive an annual salary.
2. The President shall receive a special annual allowance.
3. The Vice-President shall receive a special allowance for every day on which he acts as President.
4. The judges chosen under Article 31, other than members of the Court, shall receive compensation for each day on which they exercise their functions.
5. These salaries, allowances, and compensation shall be fixed by the General Assembly. They may not be decreased during the term of office.
6. The salary of the Registrar shall be fixed by the General Assembly on the proposal of the Court.
7. Regulations made by the General Assembly shall fix the conditions under which re-tirement pensions may be given to members of the Court and to the Registrar, and the conditions under which members of the Court and the Registrar shall have their travelling expenses refunded.
8. The above salaries, allowances, and compensation shall be free of all taxation.

Article 33

The expenses of the Court shall be borne by the United Nations in such a manner as shall be decided by the General Assembly.

CHAPTER II - COMPETENCE OF THE COURT

Article 34

1. Only states may be parties in cases before the Court.
2. The Court, subject to and in conformity with its Rules, may request of public international organizations information relevant to cases before it, and shall receive such information presented by such organizations on their own initiative.
3. Whenever the construction of the constituent instrument of a public international organization or of an international convention adopted thereunder is in question in a case before the Court, the Registrar shall so notify the public international organization concerned and shall communicate to it copies of all the written proceedings.

Article 35

1. The Court shall be open to the states parties to the present Statute.
2. The conditions under which the Court shall be open to other states shall, subject to the special provisions contained in treaties in force, be laid down by the Security Council, but in no case shall such conditions place the parties in a position of inequality before the Court.
3. When a state which is not a Member of the United Nations is a party to a case, the Court shall fix the amount which that party is to contribute towards the expenses of the Court. This provision shall not apply if such state is bearing a share of the expenses of the Court

Article 36

1. The jurisdiction of the Court comprises all cases which the parties refer to it and all matters specially provided for in the Charter of the United Nations or in treaties and conventions in force.
2. The states parties to the present Statute may at any time declare that they recognize as compulsory ipso facto and without special agreement, in relation to any other state accepting the same obligation, the jurisdiction of the Court in all legal disputes concerning:
a. the interpretation of a treaty;
b. any question of international law;
c. the existence of any fact which, if established, would constitute a breach of an international obligation;
d. the nature or extent of the reparation to be made for the breach of an international obligation.
3. The declarations referred to above may be made unconditionally or on condition of reciprocity on the part of several or certain states, or for a certain time.
4. Such declarations shall be deposited with the Secretary-General of the United Nations, who shall transmit copies thereof to the parties to the Statute and to the Registrar of the Court.
5. Declarations made under Article 36 of the Statute of the Permanent Court of International Justice and which are still in force shall be deemed, as between the parties to the present Statute, to be acceptances of the compulsory jurisdiction of the International Court of Justice for the period which they still have to run and in accordance with their terms.
6. In the event of a dispute as to whether the Court has jurisdiction, the matter shall be settled by the decision of the Court.

Article 37

Whenever a treaty or convention in force provides for reference of a matter to a tribunal to have been instituted by the League of Nations, or to the Permanent Court of International Justice, the matter shall, as between the parties to the present Statute, be referred to the International Court of Justice.

Article 38

1. The Court, whose function is to decide in accordance with international law such disputes as are submitted to it, shall apply:
a. international conventions, whether general or particular, establishing rules expressly recognized by the contesting states;
b. international custom, as evidence of a general practice accepted as law;
c. the general principles of law recognized by civilized nations;
d. subject to the provisions of Article 59, judicial decisions and the teachings of the most highly qualified publicists of the various nations, as subsidiary means for the determination of rules of law.
2. This provision shall not prejudice the power of the Court to decide a case *ex aequo et bono*, if the parties agree thereto.

CHAPTER III - PROCEDURE

Article 39

1. The official languages of the Court shall be French and English. If the parties agree that the case shall be conducted in French, the judgment shall be delivered in French. If the parties agree that the case shall be conducted in English, the judgment shall be delivered in English.
2. In the absence of an agreement as to which language shall be employed, each party may, in the pleadings, use the language which it prefers; the decision of the Court shall be given in French and English. In this case the Court shall at the same time determine which of the two texts shall be considered as authoritative.
3. The Court shall, at the request of any party, authorize a language other than French or English to be used by that party.

Article 40

1. Cases are brought before the Court, as the case may be, either by the notification of the special agreement or by a written application addressed to the Registrar. In either case the subject of the dispute and the parties shall be indicated.
2. The Registrar shall forthwith communicate the application to all concerned.
3. He shall also notify the Members of the United Nations through the Secretary-General, and also any other states entitled to appear before the Court.

Article 41

1. The Court shall have the power to indicate, if it considers that circumstances so require, any provisional measures which ought to be taken to preserve the respective rights of either party.
2. Pending the final decision, notice of the measures suggested shall forthwith be given to the parties and to the Security Council.

Article 42

1. The parties shall be represented by agents.
2. They may have the assistance of counsel or advocates before the Court.
3. The agents, counsel, and advocates of parties before the Court shall enjoy the privileges and immunities necessary to the independent exercise of their duties.

Article 43

1. The procedure shall consist of two parts: written and oral.
2. The written proceedings shall consist of the communication to the Court and to the parties of memorials, counter-memorials and, if necessary, replies; also all papers and documents in support.
3. These communications shall be made through the Registrar, in the order and within the time fixed by the Court.
4. A certified copy of every document produced by one party shall be communicated to the other party.
5. The oral proceedings shall consist of the hearing by the Court of witnesses, experts, agents, counsel, and advocates.

Article 44

1. For the service of all notices upon persons other than the agents, counsel, and advocates, the Court shall apply direct to the government of the state upon whose territory the notice has to be served.
2. The same provision shall apply whenever steps are to be taken to procure evidence on the spot.

Article 45

The hearing shall be under the control of the President or, if he is unable to preside, of the Vice-President; if neither is able to preside, the senior judge present shall preside.

Article 46

The hearing in Court shall be public, unless the Court shall decide otherwise, or unless the parties demand that the public be not admitted .

Article 47

1. Minutes shall be made at each hearing and signed by the Registrar and the President.
2. These minutes alone shall be authentic.

Article 48

The Court shall make orders for the conduct of the case, shall decide the form and time in which each party must conclude its arguments, and make all arrangements connected with the taking of evidence.

Article 49

The Court may, even before the hearing begins, call upon the agents to produce any document or to supply any explanations. Formal note shall be taken of any refusal.

Article 50

The Court may, at any time, entrust any individual, body, bureau, commission, or other organization that it may select, with the task of carrying out an enquiry or giving an expert opinion.

Article 51

During the hearing any relevant questions are to be put to the witnesses and experts under the conditions laid down by the Court in the rules of procedure referred to in Article 30.

Article 52

After the Court has received the proofs and evidence within the time specified for the purpose, it may refuse to accept any further oral or written evidence that one party may desire to present unless the other side consents.

Article 53

1. Whenever one of the parties does not appear before the Court, or fails to defend its case, the other party may call upon the Court to decide in favour of its claim.
2. The Court must, before doing so, satisfy itself, not only that it has jurisdiction in accordance with Articles 36 and 37, but also that the claim is well founded in fact and law.

Article 54

1. When, subject to the control of the Court, the agents, counsel, and advocates have completed their presentation of the case, the President shall declare the hearing closed.
2. The Court shall withdraw to consider the judgment.
3. The deliberations of the Court shall take place in private and remain secret.

Article 55

1. All questions shall be decided by a majority of the judges present.
2. In the event of an equality of votes, the President or the judge who acts in his place shall have a casting vote.

Article 56

1. The judgment shall state the reasons on which it is based.
2. It shall contain the names of the judges who have taken part in the decision.

Article 57

If the judgment does not represent in whole or in part the unanimous opinion of the judges, any judge shall be entitled to deliver a separate opinion.

Article 58

The judgment shall be signed by the President and by the Registrar. It shall be read in open court, due notice having been given to the agents.

Article 59

The decision of the Court has no binding force except between the parties and in respect of that particular case.

Article 60

The judgment is final and without appeal. In the event of dispute as to the meaning or scope of the judgment, the Court shall construe it upon the request of any party.

Article 61

1. An application for revision of a judgment may be made only when it is based upon the discovery of some fact of such a nature as to be a decisive factor, which fact was, when the judgment was given, unknown to the Court and also to the party claiming revision, always provided that such ignorance was not due to negligence.
2. The proceedings for revision shall be opened by a judgment of the Court expressly recording the existence of the new fact, recognizing that it has such a character as to lay the case open to revision, and declaring the application admissible on this ground.
3. The Court may require previous compliance with the terms of the judgment before it admits proceedings in revision.
4. The application for revision must be made at latest within six months of the discovery of the new fact.
5. No application for revision may be made after the lapse of ten years from the date of the judgment.

Article 62

1. Should a state consider that it has an interest of a legal nature which may be affected by the decision in the case, it may submit a request to the Court to be permitted to intervene.
2 It shall be for the Court to decide upon this request.

Article 63

1. Whenever the construction of a convention to which states other than those concerned in the case are parties is in question, the Registrar shall notify all such states forthwith.
2. Every state so notified has the right to intervene in the proceedings; but if it uses this right, the construction given by the judgment will be equally binding upon it.

Article 64

Unless otherwise decided by the Court, each party shall bear its own costs.

CHAPTER IV - ADVISORY OPINIONS

Article 65

1. The Court may give an advisory opinion on any legal question at the request of whatever body may be authorized by or in accordance with the Charter of the United Nations to make such a request.

2. Questions upon which the advisory opinion of the Court is asked shall be laid before the Court by means of a written request containing an exact statement of the question upon which an opinion is required, and accompanied by all documents likely to throw light upon the question.

Article 66

1. The Registrar shall forthwith give notice of the request for an advisory opinion to all states entitled to appear before the Court.

2. The Registrar shall also, by means of a special and direct communication, notify any state entitled to appear before the Court or international organization considered by the Court, or, should it not be sitting, by the President, as likely to be able to furnish information on the question, that the Court will be prepared to receive, within a time-limit to be fixed by the President, written statements, or to hear, at a public sitting to be held for the purpose, oral statements relating to the question.

3. Should any such state entitled to appear before the Court have failed to receive the special communication referred to in paragraph 2 of this Article, such state may express a desire to submit a written statement or to be heard; and the Court will decide.

4. States and organizations having presented written or oral statements or both shall be permitted to comment on the statements made by other states or organizations in the form, to the extent, and within the time-limits which the Court, or, should it not be sitting, the President, shall decide in each particular case. Accordingly, the Registrar shall in due time communicate any such written statements to states and organizations having submitted similar statements.

Article 67

The Court shall deliver its advisory opinions in open court, notice having been given to the Secretary-General and to the representatives of Members of the United Nations, of other states and of international organizations immediately concerned.

Article 68

In the exercise of its advisory functions the Court shall further be guided by the provisions of the present Statute which apply in contentious cases to the extent to which it recognizes them to be applicable.

CHAPTER V - AMENDMENT

Article 69

Amendments to the present Statute shall be effected by the same procedure as is provided by the Charter of the United Nations for amendments to that Charter, subject however to any provisions which the General Assembly upon recommendation of the Security Council may adopt concerning the participation of states which are parties to the present Statute but are not Members of the United Nations.

Article 70

The Court shall have power to propose such amendments to the present Statute as it may deem necessary, through written communications to the Secretary-General, for consideration in conformity with the provisions of Article 69.

APPENDIX C

UNIVERSAL DECLARATION OF HUMAN RIGHTS

PREAMBLE

Whereas recognition of the inherent dignity and of the equal and inalienable rights of all members of the human family is the foundation of freedom, justice and peace in the world,

Whereas disregard and contempt for human rights have resulted in barbarous acts which have outraged the conscience of mankind, and the advent of a world in which human beings shall enjoy freedom of speech and belief and freedom from fear and want has been proclaimed as the highest aspiration of the common people,

Whereas it is essential, if man is not to be compelled to have recourse, as a last resort, to rebellion against tyranny and oppression, that human rights should be protected by the rule of law,

Whereas it is essential to promote the development of friendly relations between nations,

Whereas the peoples of the United Nations have in the Charter reaffirmed their faith in fundamental human rights, in the dignity and worth of the human person and in the equal rights of men and women and have determined to promote social progress and better standards of life in larger freedom,

Whereas Member States have pledged themselves to achieve, in cooperation with the United Nations, the promotion of universal respect for and observance of human rights and fundamental freedoms,

Whereas a common understanding of these rights and freedoms is of the greatest importance for the full realization of this pledge,

Now, therefore,

The General Assembly

proclaims

This Universal Declaration of Human Rights

as a common standard of achievement for all peoples and all nations, to the end that every individual and every organ of society, keeping this Declaration constantly in mind, shall strive by teaching and education to promote respect for these rights and freedoms and by progressive measures, national and international, to secure their universal and effective recognition and observance, both among the peoples of Member States themselves and among the peoples of territories under their jurisdiction.

Article 1

All human beings are born free and equal in dignity and rights. They are endowed with reason and conscience and should act towards one another in a spirit of brotherhood.

Article 2

Everyone is entitled to all the rights and freedoms set forth in this Declaration, without distinction of any kind, such as race, colour, sex, language, religion, political or other opinion, national or social origin, property, birth or other status.
Furthermore, no distinction shall be made on the basis of the political, jurisdictional or international status of the country or territory to which a person belongs, whether it be independent, trust, non-self-governing or under any other limitation of sovereignty.

Article 3

Everyone has the right to life, liberty and security of person.

Article 4

No one shall be held in slavery or servitude; slavery and the slave trade shall be prohibited in all their forms.

Article 5

No one shall be subjected to torture or to cruel, inhuman or degrading treatment or punishment.

Article 6

Everyone has the right to recognition everywhere as a person before the law.

Article 7

All are equal before the law and are entitled without any discrimination to equal protection of the law. All are entitled to equal protection against any discrimination in violation of this Declaration and against any incitement to such discrimination.

Article 8

Everyone has the right to an effective remedy by the competent national tribunals for acts violating the fundamental rights granted him by the constitution or by law.

Article 9

No one shall be subjected to arbitrary arrest, detention or exile.

Article 10

Everyone is entitled in full equality to a fair and public hearing by an independent and impartial tribunal, in the determination of his rights and obligations and of any criminal charge against him.

Article 11

(1) Everyone charged with a penal offence has the right to be presumed innocent until proved guilty according to law in a public trial at which he has had all the guarantees necessary for his defence.

(2) No one shall be held guilty of any penal offence on account of any act or omission which did not constitute a penal offence, under national or international law, at the time when it was committed. Nor shall a heavier penalty be imposed than the one that was applicable at the time the penal offence was committed.

Article 12

No one shall be subjected to arbitrary interference with his privacy, family, home or correspondence, nor to attacks upon his honour and reputation. Everyone has the right to the protection of the law against such interference or attacks.

Article 13

(1) Everyone has the right to freedom of movement and residence within the borders of each State.

(2) Everyone has the right to leave any country, including his own, and to return to his country.

Article 14

(1) Everyone has the right to seek and to enjoy in other countries asylum from persecution.

(2) This right may not be invoked in the case of prosecutions genuinely arising from non-political crimes or from acts contrary to the purposes and principles of the United Nations.

Article 15

(1) Everyone has the right to a nationality.

(2) No one shall be arbitrarily deprived of his nationality nor denied the right to change his nationality.

Article 16

(1) Men and women of full age, without any limitation due to race, nationality or religion, have the right to marry and to found a family. They are entitled to equal rights as to marriage, during marriage and at its dissolution.

(2) Marriage shall be entered into only with the free and full consent of the intending spouses.

(3) The family is the natural and fundamental group unit of society and is entitled to protection by society and the State.

Article 17

(1) Everyone has the right to own property alone as well as in association with others.

(2) No one shall be arbitrarily deprived of his property.

Article 18

Everyone has the right to freedom of thought, conscience and religion; this right includes freedom to change his religion or belief, and freedom, either alone or in community with others and in public or private, to manifest his religion or belief in teaching, practice, worship and observance.

Article 19

Everyone has the right to freedom of opinion and expression; this right includes freedom to hold opinions without interference and to seek, receive and impart information and ideas through any media and regardless of frontiers.

Article 20

(1) Everyone has the right to freedom of peaceful assembly and association.
(2) No one may be compelled to belong to an association.

Article 21

(1) Everyone has the right to take part in the government of his country, directly or through freely chosen representatives.
(2) Everyone has the right to equal access to public service in his country.
(3) The will of the people shall be the basis of the authority of government; this will shall be expressed in periodic and genuine elections which shall be by universal and equal suffrage and shall be held by secret vote or by equivalent free voting procedures.

Article 22

Everyone, as a member of society, has the right to social security and is entitled to realization, through national effort and international co-operation and in accordance with the organization and resources of each State, of the economic, social and cultural rights indispensable for his dignity and the free development of his personality.

Article 23

(1) Everyone has the right to work, to free choice of employment, to just and favourable conditions of work and to protection against unemployment.
(2) Everyone, without any discrimination, has the right to equal pay for equal work.
(3) Everyone who works has the right to just and favourable remuneration ensuring for himself and his family an existence worthy of human dignity, and supplemented, if necessary, by other means of social protection.
(4) Everyone has the right to form and to join trade unions for the protection of his interests.

Article 24

Everyone has the right to rest and leisure, including reasonable limitation of working hours and periodic holidays with pay.

Article 25

(1) Everyone has the right to a standard of living adequate for the health and well-being of himself and of his family, including food, clothing, housing and medical care and necessary social services, and the right to security in the event of unemployment, sickness, disability, widowhood, old age or other lack of livelihood in circumstances beyond his control.

(2) Motherhood and childhood are entitled to special care and assistance. All children, whether born in or out of wedlock, shall enjoy the same social protection.

Article 26

(1) Everyone has the right to education. Education shall be free, at least in the elementary and fundamental stages. Elementary education shall be compulsory. Technical and professional education shall be made generally available and higher education shall be equally accessible to all on the basis of merit.

(2) Education shall be directed to the full development of the human personality and to the strengthening of respect for human rights and fundamental freedoms. It shall promote understanding, tolerance and friendship among all nations, racial or religious groups, and shall further the activities of the United Nations for the maintenance of peace.

(3) Parents have a prior right to choose the kind of education that shall be given to their children.

Article 27

(1) Everyone has the right freely to participate in the cultural life of the community, to enjoy the arts and to share in scientific advancement and its benefits.

(2) Everyone has the right to the protection of the moral and material interests resulting from any scientific, literary or artistic production of which he is the author.

Article 28

Everyone is entitled to a social and international order in which the rights and freedoms set forth in this Declaration can be fully realized.

Article 29

(1) Everyone has duties to the community in which alone the free and full development of his personality is possible.

(2) In the exercise of his rights and freedoms, everyone shall be subject only to such limitations as are determined by law solely for the purpose of securing due recognition and respect for the rights and freedoms of others and of meeting the just requirements of morality, public order and the general welfare in a democratic society.

(3) These rights and freedoms may in no case be exercised contrary to the purposes and principles of the United Nations.

Article 30

Nothing in this Declaration may be interpreted as implying for any State, group or person any right to engage in any activity or to perform any act aimed at the destruction of any of the rights and freedoms set forth herein.

NOTES

1. This transfer was formalized on October 25, 1971 in General Assembly Resolution 2758, which replaced the Republic of China's representation in all UN organs with the People's Republic of China.

2. After the dissolution of the USSR, the UN seat for the USSR was taken by the Russian Federation on January 31st, 1992. The Secretary-General had circulated the request of the Russian Federation to take over the USSR's seat, and seeing no opposition allowed the seating of the Russian Federation on all UN organs.

3. The ICJ can only hear cases between Members (i.e. sovereign states in the international system); it cannot hear cases from individuals, thereby making the judicial branch of the United Nations incomplete. This hole was partially covered by the introduction of the Rome Statute of 1998, which saw the formation of the International Criminal Court (ICC) which does have the authority to try individuals with respect to war crimes and crimes against humanity.

4. Reykjavik Energy Invest Press Releases, "Agreement between REI, Clinton Global Initiative and the office of the President of Iceland: Reykjavik Energy Invest contracts to invest ISK 9 billion in Africa," Reykjavik Energy Invest, http://www.rei.is/PressReleases/070929REIClintonagreement/.

5. Karekezi, Stephen and Waeni Kithyoma, "Renewable Energy in Africa: Prospects and Limits" (paper presented at The Workshop for African Energy Experts on Operationalizing the NEPAD Energy Initiative, Novotel, Dakar, Senegal, June 2-4, 2003). http://www.un.org/esa/sustdev/sdissues/energy/op/nepadkarekezi

6. U.N. General Assembly, Fifty-fifth session, "Resolution 56 (2001) [The role of diamonds in fueling conflict: breaking the link between the illicit transaction of rough diamonds and armed conflict as contribution to prevention and settlement of conflicts]," (A/RES/55/56), 29 January, 2001.

7. U.N. General Assembly, Sixty-first session, "Resolution 28 (2007) [The role of diamonds in fuelling conflict: breaking the link between the illicit transaction of rough diamonds and armed conflict as a contribution to prevention and settlement of conflicts]," (A/RES/61/28), 12 February, 2007.

8. African Heads of State and Government, "The Abuja Declaration On Roll Back Malaria in Africa," African Summit on Roll Back Malaria, Abuja, Nigeria, April 25, 2000. http://www.usaid.gov/our_work/global_health/id/malaria/publications/docs/abuja.pdf

9. World Health Organization, *Guidelines for the Treatment of Malaria*, (Geneva: WHO Press, 2006), 11.

10. World Health Organization, *Indoor Residual Spraying*, (Geneva: WHO Press, 2006), 1.

INDEX

ABOUT THE AUTHOR

Greg Hodgin was born and raised in Columbia, South Carolina, USA. He obtained a Bachelor of Science Degree in Chemistry from Emory University, a Bachelor of Arts in History and a Master of Arts in Political Science from Georgia State University. He is currently pursuing a Ph.D. in Political Science, specializing in International Relations and he is the recent founder and Executive Director of Tomorrow's Peacekeepers Today, a non-profit organization committed to merging international peace and security with human rights.

Hodgin has been participating in Model UN since 1994. He has launched the program at an Atlanta high school as well as Georgia State University and led the GSU team to Nationals. In his fifteen years in the program, he has never lost at conference.